The **THREE WORLDS** of **BALI**

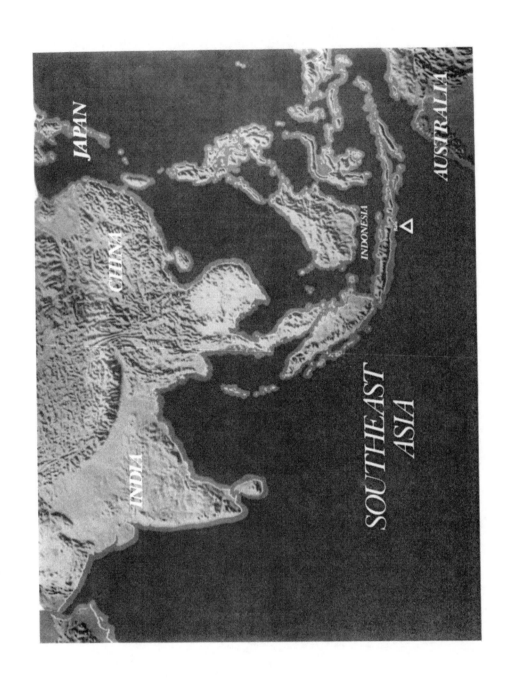

The **THREE WORLDS** of **BALI**

J. Stephen Lansing

PRAEGER

New York
Westport, Connecticut
London

Library of Congress Cataloging-in-Publication Data

Lansing, John Stephen.
  Rama's kingdom.

   Bibliography: p. 159
   Includes index.
   1. Bali (Indonesia : Province)—Civilization.
  2. Arts, Balinese—Indonesia—Bali (Province) I. Titled
  DS647.B2L26   1983   959.8'6   83-4117
  ISBN 0-275-91720-7 (alk. paper)

Library of Congress Catalog Card Number: 83-4117

ISBN: 0-275-91720-7

First published in 1983

Praeger Publishers, One Madison Avenue, New York, NY 10010
A division of Greenwood Press, Inc.

Printed in the United States of America

The paper used in this book complies with the
Permanent Paper Standard issued by the National
Information Standards Organization (Z39.48-1984).

10   9   8   7   6   5   4   3

for Marjorie Lansing

Foreword

One of the most striking, and least noted, characteristics of anthropology is that it lives so much from favored cases. University courses, professional symposia, general texts, theoretical disquisitions, even the casual conversations of colleagues thinking aloud over coffee, revert again and again to a rather small number of cultures for their examples, their arguments, and their axes of debate. They are what, empirically anyway, we have in common. One cannot count on even a first-rate scholar having heard, say, about Burmese *nat* worship or the *zadruga*, both very well studied subjects. But everyone, first-rate or fifth, knows about Australian totemism or what *kula* is.

Some of these favored cases are such because they have been the object of a classic study, or series of studies, by a single anthropologist: Malinowski and the Trobriands, Evans-Pritchard and the Nuer, Firth and the Tikopia, Boas and the Kwakiutl. Others have been very broadly "sampled" through a large number of more or less independent studies of different, but related, cultures in the same general area: Highland New Guinea, the Amazon, the American Plains; among the great civilizations, perhaps India. And yet others have gained their favored status because they have been taken to be "extreme" or "striking" examples of something instructive, if unstandard: Aztec human sacrifice, Nayar matriliny, the Israeli *kibbutz*, the League of the Iroquois.

But perhaps the most valuable of all are those cultures upon which a very wide variety of excellent ethnographers, linguists, historians, archeologists, folklorists, lawyers, students of art and religion, students of ecology and economics, even now and then a novelist or a philosopher, have worked over an extended period of time: the Navajo, the Western Pueblos, the Maya, the Australians, the Bushmen, the Bedouin—to name but some of the more striking examples. Here, intensive studies of fairly small and reasonably distinctive cultures by unusually large and extraordinarily diverse scholarly communities has led to the sort of three-dimensional record that makes for particularly rich images of (to us) exotic ways of life. One can build a sustained, wide-ranging, and multi-perspectival discussion around them—in classes, in books, in conferences, in lunchrooms—because the discussion about them has itself been so sustained, so wide-ranging, and so multi-perspectival. They are our *Drosophila* or our June days: we know them, or think we do, inch by inch, however far we remain from understanding them.

Of this rather select class of studied, and restudied and again restudied cultures, the Balinese is surely one of the most prominent. The list of names, nationalities, and disciplines this little island—1,300 square miles or so—has hosted in the name of scholarship is quite extraordinary. So is the unbroken stretch of time, roughly the 1840s to the present, over which that scholarship has gone on. So, too, is the range of subjects to which it has been addressed.

Dutchmen such as the ethnographer and customary law scholar V. E. Korn, the historian and folklorist R. E. Goris, the philologist and student of religion C. Hooykaas, all produced magisterial works in the first part of this century; as R. van Eck, F. A. Liefrinck, and H. N. van der Tuuk did on social organization, agriculture, and lexicography in the last part of the last. Even the Indologist R. Friedrich's 1847 *The Civilization and Culture of Bali*, the first general study of the island's religious and intellectual life is still useful. The Germans contributed Paul Wirz, the ethnographer of death rituals and rice cults; Walter Spies, musician, painter, and the foremost authority on Balinese dance and drama; the romantic art historians Gregor Kraus and Karl With; and even, in Vicki Baum, a talented (and accurate) ethnographic novelist. The major modern ethnographer of the island is a Mexican, Miguel Covarrubias; the most stimulating social theorist an Englishman, Gregory Bateson; the most innovative cinematographer, an Australian, John Darling. And then there are the Americans: Margaret Mead on personality development, Colin McPhee on music, Jane Belo on trance, all have produced definitive studies.

And one could name dozens of others, from the Dane L. V. Helms, who gave us our best first-hand picture of nineteenth century Balinese trade, to the Swiss U. Ramseyer, who has produced the most comprehensive study of recent Balinese art. There have been studies of the relation of Artaud's theatre of cruelty to the Balinese witch-dragon dance; of the Balinese art of temple offerings; of the history of international law in Bali; of the cultural effects of tourism; of kinship; caste; the state; witchcraft; architecture; and of calendrical calculation and musical form. No custom has been left unturned.

And the flood continues, unabated, in the present: from the United States, James Boon, Hildred Geertz, Mary Zurbuchen, Phillip McKean, Ward Keeler, Ana Daniel, Mark Poffenberger, and myself; from Holland, Henk Schulte Nordholt and H. I. R. Hinzler; from Britain, Mark and Ann

Hobart, S. O. Robson, and Anthony Forge; from Australia, P. J. Worsley; from Sweden, Ingela Gerdin; from Czechoslovakia Rudolf Mrázek; and, finally, in growing numbers, from Indonesia itself: the linguist and museologist I Gusti Ngurah Bagus, the agricultural economist I Gusti Gdé Raka, the customary law scholar Moh. Koesnoe, and the textual editors and translators I Gusti Gdé Sugriwa, I Wayan Simpen, I Putu Geria, I Gusti Ananda Kusuma, Ida Anak Agung Made Regeg—to name only some of the more prominent.

It is this extraordinary scholarly community (and my listing is not intended as an honor-role—too many fine scholars are unmentioned—but only as an image of the variety, richness, and depth of "Baliology") that J. Stephen Lansing, who has been working in Bali on and off for more than a decade, here emphatically joins. Already the author of a brief but innovative monograph—*Evil in the Morning of the World*—applying phenomenological analysis to some central Balinese religious ideas, and a number of provocative papers on various topics from kinship to irrigation, he undertakes in this book nothing less than a full-scale study of the sociological foundations of the arts in Bali.

Balinese art has, of course, been the recipient of more of the intense scholarly attention I have alluded to than perhaps any other subject. But the social roots of it have been very much less, and never extensively and systematically, investigated. The task is an enormously difficult one, not least because the sociology of art in general is so underdeveloped as to scarcely exist. Crude content analysis, vague infrastructure/superstructure arguments, even vaguer ideological or psychological deconstructions constitute, a few exceptions aside, the bulk of what has been done. It is Lansing's great virtue that he avoids these various sorts of evasions and reductions, and that he manages to face up at once to the particular quality of Balinese art, with his "sounding of the text" formulation, and to the intricacy of its relations to Balinese history, ecology, and social structure, with his stress on the centrality of the Balinese temple system in providing a material context for it.

Not everyone will agree with everything Lansing says. In so lively a scholarly world, not everyone agrees with everything anyone says; and there are those—philologers mostly—who don't agree with what anyone says. I myself remain, as he notes, unpersuaded by the "ur-village" notions of the so-called "Bali Aga theorists," and not all the statistical manipulations Lansing engages in seem to me to establish what they are intended to establish. But there is no doubt that the combination of historical, ethnographic, sociological, and, not least, aesthetic understanding Lansing displays here—in his "Indianization" discussion, in his "sounding of the text" motif, and in his fine, many-angled description, unique of its kind, of the great Eka Dasa Rudra ceremony of 1973/1979—that his book will take a permanent place in the archive of one of anthropology's most favored of favorite cases.

Clifford Geertz
Princeton, January, 1983

Acknowledgments

The initial impetus for this study of the role of art in Balinese culture came from a brief period of fieldwork in the spring and summer of 1971, funded by Wesleyan University's College of Social Studies. A subsequent study focusing on the role of art was supported by the Social Science Research Council and the Indonesian Institute for the Sciences, during the period from December 1974 to March 1976. At the conclusion of this fieldwork, I was privileged to spend a year at the Institute for Advanced Study in Princeton, nominally as an assistant to Clifford Geertz, although in truth he rendered far more assistance to me than I to him. But even after a year at the Institute, my analysis remained unfinished. The entire manuscript went through several further revisions before reaching its present state, as I tried to rethink the implications of the concept of the "sounding of the texts" for understanding the nature of Balinese civilization.

If the process of analysis has been prolonged and arduous, it has also been enormously rewarding. In 1979, the Center for Visual Anthropology of the University of Southern California provided me with the opportunity to return to Bali to make a documentary film about the Eka Dasa Rudra ceremony, and in the process convince myself once more that something so marvelous as Bali really exists.

I am greatly indebted to the Faculty of Letters of Udayana University in Bali and Dr. Gusti Ngurah Bagus, chairman of the departments of anthropology and linguistics, for support and inspiration over the past 11 years. It was a privilege to reside in the villages of Sukawati and Sanur, where among the many people who helped me I must especially thank Anak Agung Gde Poetra, Jero Wilajah, Ida Bagus Beretha, Ida Bagus Ktut Sudiasa, I Made Sanggra, I Wayan Wija, and Ida Pedanda Made.

I am also indebted to several colleagues for reading drafts of the manuscript and making suggestions: Alton Becker, Eugene Cooper, Nicholas Dirks, Clifford Geertz, Alicia Gonzalez, Ursula Koch, Alexander Moore, and Gary Seaman. Aram Yengoyan, Judith Becker, Mary Zurbuchen, Richard Wallis, and Andrew Toth provided help and inspiration. Debra Kumagawa and Norma Binkley cheerfully retyped the whole manuscript several times, "for which relief, much thanks!". Thanks, too, to the Netherlands Royal Institute of Anthropology and Linguistics for providing us the photographs that appear on pages 43, 44, 46, 47, and 48. Gordon Powell and Ron Chambers of Praeger have forever endeared themselves to me by the care they have taken in preparing—creating?—this book. Roger D. Abrahams and Jerome Rothenberg have shown me new ways to think about Balinese texts and performances. Finally, I must thank Barbara Myerhoff, who contributed immeasurably to my understanding of the meaning of "sounding the texts", and Philip McKean, who taught me to be an anthropologist, and whose book this is.

Contents

Foreword   *Clifford Geertz*   vii

Acknowledgments   xi

1. Introduction   1

2. The Indianization of Bali   15

3. The Three Worlds   51

4. The Sounding of the Texts   75

5. Village Temple Systems   93

6. Bali Aga: The Order of Time   113

7. Eka Dasa Rudra: Cycles of the Middle World   129

    Conclusion: Vehicles of the Imagination   143

Notes   149

Bibliography   159

Index   165

About the Author   171

The THREE WORLDS of BALI

1
Introduction

... and all the place is peopled with sweet airs.
The light clear element which the isle wears
Is heavy with the scent of lemon-flowers,
Which floats like mist laden with unseen showers.
                        Percy Bysshe Shelley
                        Epipsychidion

In 1937 Margaret Mead returned to New York after two year's residence in a remote peasant village in the mountains of Bali. Shortly after her return, she wrote the following impression of village life:

> Here was an almost incredible business; day and night, the roads were full of people walking with a light and swinging step under heavy loads; the air was never empty of music, even in the small hours before the dawn; and it was not mere woodland piping but complicated orchestral music which bore witness to many hours of concentrated rehearsal. Upon the hundreds of stone altars of Bali, there lay not merely a fruit and a flower, placed as a visible offering to the many gods, but hundreds of finely wrought and elaborately conceived offerings made of palm leaf and flowers, twisted, folded, stitched, embroidered, brocaded into myriad traditional forms and fancies. There were flowers made of sugar and combined into representations of the rainbow, and swords and spears cut from the snow-white fat of sacrificial pigs. The whole world was patterned, from the hillsides elaborately terraced to give the maximum rice yield, to the air which was shot through with music, the temple gates festooned with temporary palm-leaf arras over their permanent carved facade, to the crowds of people who, as they lounged, watching an opera or clustered around two fighting cocks, composed themselves into a frieze .... Their lives were packed with intricate and formal delights.[1]

1

Anthropologists who have lived for extended periods in peasant villages are typically more apt to describe their experiences as an ordeal rather than as a sort of movable feast. But Mead's exuberance was echoed by many observers, from artists and dancers to archaeologists and anthropologists. "The Balinese may be described as a nation of artists," wrote Geoffrey Gorer in 1936.[2] Antonin Artaud waxed lyrical in praise of the Balinese theater, apparently after witnessing a performance by a village troupe at the Paris Exposition.[3] A more informed account was written by Jane Belo, an anthropologist who lived for years on Bali and wrote several excellent technical monographs on Balinese religion. In an introduction to a collection of essays on "Traditional Balinese Culture," Belo described the rhythm of village life:

> The average Balinese man worked hard in the ricefields all day, and the women carried water from the spring, went to market, cooked, swept the house-court, and in their spare time created beautiful textiles on the hand loom or prepared on special pedestals the festive offerings of cakes and flowers and palm leaf fringes for the gods. Both men and women looked after little children. When the men assembled at night, after the day's work, to practise in the continually ongoing rehearsals of the gamelan orchestra they carried or held in their laps the babies born to them in the year or so past, and thus the little children received their first grounding in the complex rhythms of Balinese music. When the performance of a play, perhaps with hand-carved masks, was being prepared for the next celebration of a temple's calendrical festival, the small children sat in rows at the very front of the onlookers, and when a shadow play was given in the village the small children sitting in the front rows would doze off and go to sleep for awhile, only to wake up, alert and bright-eyed, for the enactment of the most exciting scenes of the Hindu epics, the Mahābhārata and the Rāmāyana, when gods appear, heroes and demons clash, or the more recent versions of old Javanese and Balinese tales of the witch and her evil pupils wreaking havoc in the land. Painting and sculpture both in stone and in wood were practised by professionals and amateurs who could sell their products, always lively and curious, to the tourists. The temples were decorated with panels of carved stone in a design so well known by the villagers that two men could start the decorative motif at opposite ends of the strip of wall and meet in the middle, without any preliminary sketch and without breaking the continuity of the whole.[4]

Visitors, said Belo, were "always impressed with the relentless creativity of the Balinese."[5] In the preface to the book *Dance and Drama in Bali*, Arthur Waley asked, "What has made Bali a special case?"[6] Margaret Mead posed this question more formally in an essay in which she asked, "What is the difference between the society in which the arts are an integral part of everyday life, enriching and enhancing it, and the society in which the arts are almost wholly dispensed with?" Mead contrasted the Balinese with the Lepchas of Sikkim:

> Like the Balinese, the Lepchas are quite a well-fed people, although both have to work hard to produce a surplus. This surplus, however, the Lepchas simply eat up and drink up in conviviality, while the Balinese consume their surplus in far more complicated ways, in rice cakes which the village women have shaped into a goddess, in gold leaf in square yards over cremation towers which will glitter for an hour above the treetops and then be dismantled and burned, in feeding the members of five orchestras to play at once for one ceremony.[7]

A "SPECIAL CASE"

Bali is an island in the Indonesian archipelago, 172 miles long (east-west) by 102 miles across (north-south) at its widest points, just east of Java and a few degrees south of the Equator. The climate is monsoonal, and the natural vegetation is rain forest. A chain of active volcanoes runs along the longer (east-west) axis, creating a rain shadow to the north but ensuring plentiful rainfall along the southern coastal plains. Sometime in the first millenium A.D., a civilization emerged in the alluvial plains of the south based on wet-rice agriculture. The scene, as Clifford Geertz aptly observed, is Lilliputian in scale—the region is bounded to the north by the chain of volcanoes, to the west by thickly forested land unsuitable for agriculture, and to the east by an arid peninsula. "From the highest line of intensive wet-rice agriculture (±2000 feet) to the shore is only fifteen to twenty miles in the west, twenty to twenty-five in the center, and ten to fifteen in the east. . . . If ever there was a forcing ground for the growth of a singular civilization, this snug little amphitheater was it; and if what was produced turned out to be a rather special little orchid, perhaps we should not be altogether surprised."[8]

Geertz sees the "continual explosion of competitive display" in "myth, rite, art and architecture" as a consequence of the nature of the Balinese state. Like all "classical" Southeast Asian civilizations, Balinese civilization drew its initial inspiration from Indian (Hindu-Buddhist) theories of divine kingship. The Balinese word for civilization, *negara*, is a Sanskrit loanword and actually means "royal capital." The legitimacy of a Balinese ruler derived from his ability to construct a capital which was an "exemplary center," a

> microcosm of the supernatural order—'an image of . . . the universe on a smaller scale'—and the material embodiment of political order. It is

not just the nucleus, the engine, or the pivot of the state, it *is* the state. The equation of the seat of rule with the dominion of rule, which the negara concept expresses, is more than an accidental metaphor; it is a statement of a controlling political idea—namely, that by the mere act of providing a model, a paragon, a faultless image of civilized existence, the court shapes the world around it into at least a rough approximation of its own excellence. The ritual life of the court, and in fact the court generally, is thus paradigmatic, not merely reflective, of social order. What it is reflective of, the priests declare, is supernatural order, the 'timeless Indian world of the gods' upon which men should, in strict proportion to their status, seek to pattern their lives.[9]

The relationship of this concept of the state to the "continual outpouring of symbolic forms" becomes clear through Geertz's description of the continuous competition among would-be Universal Monarchs to establish themselves and their courts as "the center of centers, the axis of the world."

The whole of the negara-court life, the traditions that organized it, the extractions that supported it, the privileges that accompanied it— was essentially directed towards what power was; and what power was was what kings were. Particular kings came and went, "poor passing facts" anonymized in titles, immobilized in ritual, and annihilated in bonfires. But what they represented, the model-and-copy conception of order, remained unaltered . . . . The driving aim of higher politics was to construct a state by constructing a king. The more consummate the king, the more exemplary the center. The more exemplary the center, the more actual the realm.[10]

But as Geertz goes on to observe, the "landscape, not only in Bali but throughout Southeast Asia, and over the course of at least fifteen hundred years, was dotted with universal monarchs, each represented, in the declamations of his cult, as the core and pivot of the universe, yet each quite aware that he was emphatically not alone in such representation . . . . Kings were all Incomparable, but some were more Incomparable than others." Thus the "struggle for power" became a "continual explosion of competitive display."[11]

The stupendous cremations, tooth fillings, temple dedications, pilgrimages, and blood sacrifices, mobilizing hundreds and even thousands of people and great quantities of wealth, were not means to political ends: they were the ends themselves, they were what the state was for. Court ceremonialism was the driving force of court politics . . . .[12]

Geertz concludes that "the state drew its force, which was real enough, from its imaginative energies, its semiotic capacity to make inequality enchant."[13] He shows that the genealogical structure of Balinese kingship led to a proliferation of tiny courts in the "snug little amphitheater" of South Bali, each striving to become an exemplary center, each therefore compelled to mount a continuous quasi-liturgical symbolic display.

Geertz's analysis greatly advances our understanding of the Balinese state, but it is not entirely satisfactory as an explanation for the "continual explosion of competitive display in myth, rite, art and architecture." The difficulty is that the end of the classical era and the elimination of the competition among courts did not cause a halt (or even an appreciable diminution) in the "outpouring of symbolic forms." The Dutch conquered northern Bali in the late nineteenth century, and in the first decade of the twentieth century invaded the south. The major courts were not merely defeated, they were obliterated. In the leading palaces of Klungkung and Badung, the ruler and his followers chose to enact the Puputan—the Finish—the entire court, princes, princesses, priests, and courtiers walking deliberately into gunfire, and the survivors fatally stabbing themselves with ceremonial swords. Their palaces were bombarded and razed to the ground. None of the larger courts of Bali escaped this destruction. But the overthrow and obliteration of the classical states of Bali paradoxically had remarkably little effect on Balinese culture. If one compares ethnographic accounts from the period before the Dutch conquest with accounts written after, it is abundantly clear that almost nothing changed. Even the great mass spectacles continued. In Chapter 7 we will consider the Eka Dasa Rudra mass ceremonial held in 1979, which was arguably larger and more intricate than any of the recorded rituals performed by the monarchs of the nineteenth century. If we are to find the roots of this special orchid, we must look beyond the classical states to discover the "imaginative energies from which they drew their force."

THE ROLE OF TEMPLES

One afternoon in 1975, returning from a visit to a distant village, I was surprised to see a crowd of several hundred Balinese clustered around the ancient royal temple of the former kingdom of Sukawati. In the eighteenth century, Sukawati was a powerful court, but by the late nineteenth century it had shrunk to the status of a vassal princedom and was conquered by a neighboring prince, its palace burned to the ground. I spoke to an elderly gentleman engaged in supervising the adornment of a *padmasana* (carved stone shrine in the form of a throne) with flower offerings and learned that he had lived in another part of the island all his life, but that his grandfathers had been *kaula kawisuda*, or hereditary minor courtiers, of the Sukawati court. The Balinese concept of reincarnation holds that people are ordinarily reborn into their own families—as their own descendants—and the old man believed himself to be a reincarnation of his great-grandfather. Hence in a former life he had been *kaula kawisuda* to the court of Sukawati.

On the following day, he and several hundred other reincarnated subjects of the former kingdom of Sukawati assembled at the temple, and the spirits of the former lords of Sukawati were invited to descend into the gold-and-flower-bedecked *padmasana*. The shade of the last ruler duly appeared and spoke to his subjects through a medium in a trance. In a series of dramatic performances, the former glories of the kingdom were remembered. The court of Sukawati, past and present, living and dead, reconstituted itself in a magnificent two-day pageant and then vanished; crowds, priests, and artists returned to their respective homes to reappear in another year for the next royal temple festival.

Such performances are not unusual; indeed, they are entirely normal and predictable. As Geertz himself shows in *Negara: The Balinese Theater State in the Nineteenth Century*, every Balinese palace was laid out in the form of a temple, with the king's quarters in the innermost (and hence most sacred) corner. Every ruling dynasty had its own "State Temples," where past and present members of the courts regularly gathered to make offerings to their gods. The Balinese concept of reincarnation and of the cyclical nature of time helped to create a sense of historical continuity. In the center of each court was a temple and a ruler who aspired to be a god. The Dutch conquest destroyed many palaces but left most royal temples intact, and the shades of kings and their courts continue to visit those temples on calendrically determined dates. Their wrath is likely to fall on any reincarnated former subjects who fail to welcome their visits to the temples by making the appropriate offerings. The apparition of ghostly kingdoms periodically reappearing for gorgeous festivals, and then abruptly vanishing, is a regular occurrence. Thus, in a sense, Balinese courts were actually temples—and as temples, they continue to exist. But of what significance are temples?

Part of the argument of this book hinges on the proposition that Balinese civilization was primarily rooted not in the courts but in networks of temples. This argument will be developed at length in the chapters to follow, but very briefly, it proceeds like this:

"Civilization" is best defined not in terms of its attributes (large, dense populations, monumental architecture, writing and calendars, and so forth), but rather in terms of its intrinsic structure: complex organizational systems, or institutions, that extend beyond the boundaries of individual villages or communities to link together whole regions. These institutions serve a variety of functions: political, economic, religious, and social. In the West the growth of such institutions was synonymous with the growth of cities, from which our word "civilization" derives. But in Bali the development of complex regional institutions did not lead to the formation of cities. The evolution of Balinese civilization followed a very different course, in which institutional structures were dispersed along networks of temples, which managed everything from the control of irrigation to the rituals of a Balinese version of the Hindu caste system.

A typical Balinese village contains several dozen temples, each belonging to one of the regional institutional systems: farming temples, water temples, caste temples, village and state temples, and so forth. Altogether there are upward of 20,000 temples on Bali! These temples do not merely symbolize institutions; the cycles of temple festivals and rituals actually determine the activities of the institution represented by the temple. Thus, for example, water temples schedule the opening and closing of irrigation canals by means of their ritual calendars, and the coordination of water use for entire regions is accomplished via the institutional links between temples. In similar ways, as we shall see, village and caste temples regulate the activities of their respective organizations.

But having said this, we are confronted immediately with a seeming paradox. Balinese temples are not permanent buildings filled with busy administrators managing a theocratic state. Instead, they are little more than open-air theaters—walled rectangular courtyards without roofs, with a few shrines, and with altars in the uphill corner. Most of the time they are empty, awaiting the next "activation date" when they will be filled with offerings and performances for a few days, then emptied once again. The "practical" affairs of the temple/institution are indeed planned and executed during these festivals, but they seem almost incidental to the gorgeous ceremonies which are the main business of the festivals, in the same way that ceremony and spectacle were the main business of the classical Balinese states. The same version of cosmological order that gave shape to the Indic kingships of Bali, and made the palace into a temple and the king into a god, makes the thousands of temple courtyards fit together into organized, functioning institutional orders. Temples form links between the human world and the unseen worlds of Indic cosmology, which postulates that events in the human (Middle) world are continuously influenced by the upper worlds of gods and ancestral spirits and by the lower world of demonic powers. The success of human undertakings, literally from birth to death, depends upon keeping the forces of these two worlds in balance, which is the primary purpose of every temple festival.

The ability of the temple system to provide an institutional system governing the basic affairs of social life thus depends on the success of temple festivals in persuasively articulating this cosmological vision in which the links to the other worlds are seen as crucial for carrying out a range of projects from growing rice to raising children. Temple festivals must activate the imagination to make the unseen appear real and significant, to make the cosmology a vivid reality.

ART AND THE IMAGINATION

What the Balinese show us, both by means of their example, and (as we shall see) in their formal aesthetics, is that we have vastly underestimated the significance of art as a vehicle for shaping and molding the imagination, and thereby giving pattern and meaning to the world. This Balinese view of art, which will be explored in detail in Chapter 4, contrasts sharply with the modern Western view of art, as expressed both in the mainstream traditions of aesthetics and art history and in the more specialized and recent studies of art by anthropologists.

Some years ago, Paul Kristeller wrote a definitive essay, "The Modern System of the Arts," in which he observed that "the various arts are certainly as old as human civilization, but the manner in which we are accustomed to group them and to assign them a place in our scheme of life and culture is comparatively recent."[14] The original Greek term for art was *techne*, "the shaping of the materials of nature for the use or enjoyment of man."[15] Thus, as Kristeller notes, "the Greek term for Art (techne) and its Latin equivalent (ars) do not specifically denote the "fine arts" in the modern sense, but were applied to all kinds of human activities which we would call crafts or sciences."[16] This broad definition of art continued through the Medieval period and the Renaissance. "For Aquinas shoemaking, cooking and juggling, grammar and arithmetic are no less and in no other senses *artes* than painting and sculpture, poetry and music, which latter are never grouped together, not even as imitative arts."[17] As late as 1690, "the definition of 'Fine Arts' for Perrault included optics and mechanics with eloquence, poetry, music, architecture, sculpture and painting."[18] Kristeller identifies the crystallization of the modern concept of Fine Arts and its subsequent popularization in Europe with the publication of Diderot's *Encyclopedie* in 1751: "The term Beaux Arts, and 'Art' in the new sense, found its way into the dictionaries of the French language that had ignored it before."[19]

At almost precisely the same moment, the modern concept of aesthetics was defined by a German philosopher, Alexander Baumgarten. But, as Kristeller observes, "the original meaning of the term aesthetics, as coined by Baumgarten, which has been well nigh forgotten by now, is the theory of sensuous knowledge, as a counterpart to logic as a theory of intellectual knowledge."[20] This original link between art and understanding is also reflected in an engraving for the *Encyclopedie*, printed in Weimar in 1769: "It represents the tree of the arts and sciences as given in the text of D'Alembert's Discours, putting the visual arts, poetry and music with their subdivisions under the general branch of the imagination."[21] Kant was the first philosopher to include aesthetics and the philosophical theory of the arts as an integral part of his philosophical system. In an interesting footnote to the *Critique of Pure Reason*, he argues against the use of the term aesthetics for the criticism of taste (*Kritik des Geschmacks*), which he says is based on a mistaken hope of "controlling the critical judgement of the beautiful by means of the principles of reason, and elevating these rules into a science." Instead, Kant defines aesthetics as "the critical analysis of perception."[22]

But his arguments were not heeded, and aesthetics became grounded in the hermeneutic tradition of Western scholarship. Thus, aesthetic analysis has become the analysis of the processes by which artworks become invested with meaning, the analysis of form, style and composition. Rather than a theory of sensuous knowledge or of the role of the imagination, or the critical analysis of perception, aesthetics came to be defined as "the critical judgment of the beautiful." The separation of the fine arts—poetry, music, sculpture, painting, and architecture—from the "folk" and "popular" arts grew increasingly significant, and the domain of art became increasingly restricted. Thus, in a recent monograph on "Aesthetic Anthropology," Jacques Maquet asks, "Is aesthetic sensibility universal?" and "Has Art a non-Western meaning?"[23] In attempting to answer these questions, Maquet points to the existence in non-Western cultures of objects without practical use, which have "an exclusive visual function".

> In traditional Africa there were the cups carved in the shape of human heads by Kuba craftsmen for their wealthy nobility (they were cups, but so elaborate as carvings that they were rather looked at than used to drink palm wine). There were the miniaturized baskets made by the aristocratic ladies of the Tutsi class in Rwanda. There were the golden pendants of the Ashanti and other Akan people, the small brass figurines made in Dahomey.[24]

For Maquet, aesthetics is not the analysis of perception, or sensuous knowledge, or the imagination; instead, it is defined by a particular perceptual attitude, which he terms "contemplation." Art objects are then defined by their ability to "stimulate aesthetic awareness better than other artifacts and even to sustain aesthetic contemplation."[25] Hence the role of specialists in art, "aestheticians, art historians, critics, psychologists," who "attempt to delineate as precisely as possible what features in a sculpture or painting stimulate aesthetic awareness, what constitutes their aesthetic quality."[26]

This attitude toward art does indeed seem to underlie our experience of art in the last two centuries in the West. In concert halls, galleries, museums, and theaters we contemplate the "Fine Arts". If we are inclined to accept the inclusion of architecture as a Fine Art, we also learn to contemplate buildings! But it is perfectly obvious that this attitude toward art, despite its pretensions to universality, is a phenomenon of recent European culture; painting, music, sculpture, and the other arts did not originate in the eighteenth century, although museums, picture galleries, and concert halls did. If we inquire into the situation of the arts in earlier times, clearly their usual setting was for the most part religious. Indeed, the emancipation of the arts from religion is one of the major themes of modernist aesthetics. We applaud the emergence of landscapes in Renaissance painting, the birth of secular literature, of nonliturgical music—the gradual substitution of secular themes and subjects for religious ones in each of the arts. In quite a fundamental sense, our aesthetics has been a tool for disentangling art from religion. It is of course conceivable that modernist aesthetics is indeed a step forward, as its champions proclaim, that the Fine Arts have at last been liberated from their religious background. But in a sense, the whole issue of the claims of modernist aesthetics is beside the point once we turn our attention away from the modern West to cultures such as Bali, where religion and art are inextricably linked. What could conceivably be gained by attempting to discover Pure Form in Balinese art by excising its religious content? Surely it is precisely the relationship of art to religion which must be the first focus of analysis. For such a study it is not modernist aesthetics, but aesthetics as it was understood by Kant and Baumgarten that promises to provide useful tools.

ART AND CULTURE

If we define aesthetics not as the "critical judgment of the beautiful," but in its original sense as the "theory of sensuous knowledge, the role of the imagination, the critical analysis of perception," then art ceases to be a peripheral subject and assumes a central position in our understanding of culture as the means by which the imagination transcends the limitations of individual minds and becomes a shared vision. Art is a vehicle for the imagination, created by individuals but shared as a cultural tradition. Consciously manipulating the symbolic vehicles of perception—words, colors, and music—in traditions evolved over generations, the arts are the most sophisticated tools of the human imagination. Art actively shapes our perceptions of reality and then allows us to reflect upon that shaping. Art is the manipulation of sound into music, of color into image, of words into structured tales—the symbolic patterning of perception. From a biological standpoint, it could well be argued that art is the highest faculty of the human mind—the deliberate, reflexive ordering of perception, the conscious construction of a mode of experience. From this perspective, it is not surprising that art and religion are almost invariably closely linked. Art is used to express a culture's most profound knowledge of the world, presumably because the arts provide the tools for the most precise and imaginatively compelling articulation of such knowledge.

Art assumes this role only within the context of the modern anthropological theory of culture—the realization that the human world is imaginatively constructed. George Stocking sees the genesis of this concept in Franz Boas's odyssey from physics to psychophysics to anthropology, beginning with his doctoral dissertation on Eskimo perceptions of the color of sea water.

> Quantitative variation in the object did not evoke corresponding variation in the subject. Boas was later to repeat the experience on the linguistic level, when the Northwest Coast informants he discovered that sounds considered the same by a speaker of one language might be heard as completely different by speakers of another, and vice versa, as each perceived in the discourse of the other the distinctions appropriate to his own.[27]

Reflecting on Boas's 1889 paper "On Alternating Sounds," Stocking observes that it "foreshadows a great deal of modern anthropological thought on 'culture.' At least by implication, it sees cultural phenomena in terms of the imposition of conventional meaning on the flux of experience. It sees them as historically conditioned and transmitted by the learning process." As Boas discovered, "the seeing eye is the organ of tradition."[28]

Boas's formulation has been strengthened by discoveries in the neurosciences, psychology, and linguistics, as well as anthropology. As one neuroscientist put it, "reality is a construction of the central nervous system." We learn to see, to hear, to recognize, to understand according to culturally defined patterns. Much of this cultural shaping of perception occurs below the level of conscious thought—sounds reaching the ears, for example, are subjected to a filtering process analogous to Fourier transforms so that the mind "hears" only what it has learned to be potentially meaningful. Thus, Boas's original experiments on the role of "culture" in shaping perception have been supported by our developing picture of the nature of human intelligence. The mind integrates perceptual information through cultural "filters" and constructs for itself a representation of the outer world shaped by the dictates of a particular culture. Thus, as Marshall Sahlins recently observed, the modern anthropological concept of culture

> takes as the distinctive quality of man not that he must live in a
> material world, a circumstance he shares with all organisms, but that
> he does so according to a meaningful scheme of his own devising . . . a
> definite symbolic scheme which is never the only one possible.[29]

But while human minds are individual and private, culture as it is thus defined is plural and intersubjective, a shared way of experiencing the world. It is in this context that an anthropological aesthetics may take its place as the study of the vehicles of the imagination, the cultural traditions by which perception is molded into symbolic images that help to define a world.

It is from this perspective that we will attempt to understand Bali: a tropical island where the festivals of 20,000 temples provide opportunities for the arts to bring to life the intricate visions of Indic cosmology. It will be argued that the Hindu-Buddhist civilization of Bali was brought to the island by the arts, spread by means of the arts, and is today sustained by the arts.

PLAN OF THE BOOK

The first civilization to emerge in Bali was inspired by Indian models. To understand how this civilization came into being, it is necessary to consider the more general question of the reasons for the spread of "Indianized" civilizations in Southeast Asia. In the first millenium A.D., Bali was only one among hundreds of Indic kingdoms that shared many similar features. Hence, Chapter 2 considers the origin and growth of Balinese civilization from the perspective of the general process of "Indianization" in Southeast Asia by using archaeological and historical sources. Why did these "Indic" kingdoms come into being?

Chapter 3 attempts to define the nature of Balinese civilization in terms of the operations of temple networks. We consider the general nature of Balinese temples, their relationship to the arts, and the role of specific temple networks in organizing Balinese society.

Chapter 4 is concerned with the place of artistic performances in Balinese culture. We consider Balinese concepts of art and aesthetics, both in terms of their significance for understanding Balinese culture and their relationship to Western theories of aesthetics and semiotics.

Chapter 5 describes the temple networks operating in most Balinese villages, arguing that the fluid nature of the social life is created by "the sounding of the texts," which constantly reshapes the social world.

Chapter 6 considers an unusual group of villages, the Bali Aga, arguing that the unique features of these villages are due to the different roles played by temples and performances.

Chapter 7 describes the great century-turning ceremony of Eka Dasa Rudra, a supreme example of the power of "the sounding of the texts" to structure the social world.

Finally, the Conclusion evaluates the role of art, and in particular the "sounding" of the texts, in the formation and development of Balinese civilization.

2
The Indianization of Bali

It would seem that mythological worlds have been built up only to be
shattered again, and that new worlds were built from the fragments.

Franz Boas

"INDIANIZATION"

In two recent review articles, I. W. Mabbett summarizes the prehistoric and historic sources bearing on the question of an "Indian
influence" in the development of Southeast Asian societies.[1] A similar
review was undertaken by Paul Wheatley in "Satyantra in Suvarnadvipa,"
and more recently by Ken Hall.[2] Each of these authors makes similar
points: there are essentially three major hypotheses that have been
advanced over the years to account for the spread of Indian influence (the
Brahmana, Ksatriya, and Waisya, respectively, to which we will return),
but the evidence by which to decide among these hypotheses is lacking.
After a "brief outline of the sources of 'Indianization' which is practically
complete," I. W. Mabbett concludes that

> it is unlikely that a prolongation of the catalogue of possible sources
> would add much to what has already been gleaned—more Indian trade
> goods, more inscriptions recording the activity of pious Hindu or
> Buddhist rulers, more unreliable Chinese second-hand accounts of
> Indian priests and Indianized "kingdoms." The purpose of extending
> the catalogue this far has been twofold. In the first place, it is to make
> quite clear that the actual process of "Indianization" is nowhere
> reliably portrayed; what is portrayed by the earliest evidence is the

15

operation of kingdoms already Indianized; and therefore the various theories that have been offered are speculation. One may seem more plausible or attractive than another, but none has been established.[3]

The hypotheses in question refer to the possible roles of Brahman priests, Ksatriya adventurers, or Waisya traders in spreading "Indian influence" into Southeast Asia. As Mabbett shows, there is actually ample evidence for the presence of them all along the trade routes of Southeast Asia in the first millenium A.D. The possibilities are endless, for conceivably Brahmans might have functioned as traders, while Ksatriyas might have been the bearers of Sanskrit culture. But over the years a range of theories has been constructed, emphasizing the role of one or another group. Majumdar[4] postulated wholesale colonization by Indian exiles. At the other extreme, J. C. van Leur[5] maintained that Indianization was wholly initiated by Southeast Asians who summoned Brahmans to their courts, creating merely a "thin and flaking glaze" of Indianized customs. Between these poles, nearly every conceivable intermediate position has been staked out,[6] but there is as yet no consensus as to which is more likely.

Is the problem simply the inadequacy of archaeological evidence, or is it, as Mabbett hints, more fundamental? Will archaeology ultimately permit us to affirm one hypothesis and reject the others?

The whole debate has so far focused exclusively on the movements of *people*: traders, princes, and Brahmans—Indians, Chinese, and Southeast Asians. However, Indianization was not, fundamentally, a movement of people, but rather of ideas. On this point the historical record is clear enough. The Indic civilizations of Southeast Asia were not the product of large-scale Indian conquests or colonization but were created by the Southeast Asians themselves. In the period between the third and thirteenth centuries A.D., hundreds of Indic kingdoms (*negara*) appeared across the length and breadth of Southeast Asia, from the plains of Cambodia and Central Java to remote corners of Borneo and highland Burma. There is no evidence that any of them was an Indian colony. Indeed, the total absence of direct Indian control is striking when we compare these Indianized states with the Sinicized kingdoms of Vietnam, where Chinese models were indeed deliberately imposed.

The term "*negara*" is itself somewhat misleading; it suggests a particular type of society, when in truth it denotes a diverse collection of societies, from the tiny coastal trading principalities of the archipelago to the great inland wet-rice kingdoms of Java and the mainland. What unites them all as *negara* is their common adoption of Indic models of kingship and social order. This adoption appears to have been voluntary on the part of the Southeast Asians, i.e., not a result of Indian conquest or forced imposition from outside (although it may well have been a matter of some segments of a Southeast Asian society imposing the new models on their fellows). What is most striking about the whole process is that it did not merely happen once or twice, but hundreds of times. Consequently, the traditional hypotheses on Indianization seem somewhat beside the point. The question is not so much who brought Indic models to Southeast Asia, but rather, why did the Southeast Asians choose to adopt them?

Let us begin by trying to define more precisely the nature of these "Indic models." How does an archaeologist recognize Indian influence? When Southeast Asians adopt a Sanskrit or Pali vocabulary, when they begin to describe themselves and their world in the idiom of Hindu/ Buddhist thought, when they create works of art or architecture that express a Hindu/Buddhist worldview in a style that shows some continuity with the sources of those traditions, these provide the tangible evidences of Indianization, and they range from fragments of stone inscriptions from Sumatran river banks to miles of sculpted friezes along Cambodian temples. For the archaeologist, such (quite dissimilar!) objects are linked as evidence of Indianization because they all signify the adoption by indigenous peoples of a partially Indian (Hindu or Buddhist) worldview. It is important to note that this does not mean simply that they were converted to one sect or another by visiting Indians. A much more sustained and significant sort of contact is evidenced, for example, by archaeological remains from the great Indian university of Nālandā, which flourished in the second half of the first millenium A.D. Nālandā was the destination of the great Chinese Buddhist travellers such as Hsüan Tsang and I Tsing, where they gathered and studied the texts that were to transform Chinese, Korean, and Japanese society. Other monks from Nālandā translated Buddhist texts into Tibetan and founded the first Himalayan monasteries. During the same period, a Javanese king of the Śailēndra dynasty, builders of Borobudur, endowed a monastery at Nālandā with the assistance of the Gupta ruler. An inscription from Nālandā recording this collaboration expresses the nature of the world-view that drew Javanese and Indian kings together as participants in a cultural system that transcended political and geographical frontiers:

We being requested by the illustrious Maharaja Bālaputradēva, the king of Suvarnadvīpa, through a messenger, have caused to be built a monastary at Nālānda....
In this religious undertaking Balavavarman, the illustrious ruler of the Vyāghratatī-mandala, acted as a messenger of the illustrious [Emperor] Dēvapāladēva. There was a king of Yavabhūmi [Java]—who was the ornament of the Śailēndra dynasty, whose lotus-feet bloomed by the luster of the jewels in the row of trembling diadems, on the heads of all the princes....

With his mind attracted by the manifold excellences of Nālandā and
through devotion to the son of Śuddhōdana [the Buddha] and having
realized that riches were fickle like the waves of a mountain stream,
he ... built there [at Nālandā] a monastery which was the abode of
the assembly of monks of good qualities, and was white with the series
of stuccoed and lofty dwellings. Having been requested King
Dēvapāladēva [the Gupta king], who was the preceptor for initiating
into widowhood the wives of all the enemies, granted five villages
[mentioned earlier], to support the monks.
As long as the ocean exists ... and as long as the Eastern and Western
mountains have their crest jewels scratched by the hooves of the horses
of the Sun, so long may this meritorious act, setting up virtues all
over the world, endure.[7]

Pursuing our question (Why did Southeast Asians choose to adopt
certain Indic concepts?), we may ask in this particular instance why a
ruler of faraway Java should take such an interest in the welfare of an
Indian monastic university. In one sense, the text provides the answer: as
an act of Buddhist piety. But this act was carried out several thousand
miles from the Javanese king's domains and what we might presume to be
his usual sphere of influence. However, the inscription is not the only
archaeological evidence of Javanese interest in Nālandā. The Director of
the Nālandā archaeological excavations notes that many small bronze
Boddhisattva images recovered from Nālandā bore a striking resemblance
to Javanese bronzes. Investigating this similarity, he found what
amounted to proof of a relationship: "Apart from the details of the form of
these images, which is very similar, the back of many of them shows a
common feature which is a small piece soldered onto the back, on which
the creed formula is engraved in Nāgarī letters."[8] Here is impressive
physical evidence of a direct cultural contact between a Southeast Asian
society and one of the centers of Indian thought. With this evidence, we
can frame a more specific question: What attracted the Southeast Asians to
Nālandā, and what did they take from it?

Historical accounts of Nālandā are based primarily on the descriptions
of Chinese travelers who were drawn to Nālandā as one of the centers of
Mahāyāna Buddhist thought, from about the sixth century onward. Their
accounts naturally stress the importance of Nālandā as a haven of
Buddhist studies, but they also demonstrate that it was indeed a sort of
monastic university, where all systems of knowledge were explored.
Hsüan Tsang provides us with a beautiful description of Nālandā in the
mid-seventh century:

The whole establishment is surrounded by a brick wall which
encloses the entire convent from without. One gate opens into the great

college, from which are separated eight other halls, standing in the middle of the Samghārāma. The richly adorned towers, and the fairy-like turrets resembling pointed hilltops, are congregated together. The observatories seem to be lost in the vapours of the morning, and the upper rooms tower above the clouds.... The Samghārāmas of India are counted by myriads but this is the most remarkable for grandeur and height. The priests belonging to the convent or strangers residing therein always reach to the number of 10,000 who all study the Great Vehicle [Mahāyāna Buddhism] as well as the works of all the eighteen rival sects of Buddhism and even ordinary works, such as the Vedas and other books, and the works of Magic or the Atharva-Veda, besides these they thoroughly investigate the "miscellaneous" works....[9]

Let us not detain Hsüan Tsang, but permit him to enter and begin his great work of translation, while we linger for a moment outside to consider the significance of those "other books" and the observatories "lost in the vapours of the morning." The period from the sixth to the tenth centuries in India saw the flowering of both mathematics and astronomy—two sciences that were closely linked, since the development of the mathematical tools of trigonometry, algebra, the decimal system, and geometry led to advances in spherical astronomy (*golapada*) and time reckoning (*kālakriyapada*).[10]

We cannot expect Buddhist travelers such as Hsüan Tsang to wax eloquent over these topics, which for them represented mere "footnotes" to the dazzling cosmological speculations of Buddhist metaphysics. Nonetheless, we have ample evidence that these footnotes were of great interest to Southeast Asians.

One such footnote is the mathematical concept of zero. Although developed by Indian mathematicians, the first historical evidence of its use occurs not in India, but in a Cambodian calendrical inscription of 604 A.D. Subsequently, zero appears in Champa (609), Java (732), and finally in India in the Bhojadeva inscriptions of Gwalior in 870 A.D.[11] It is important to note that zero does not appear as an isolated borrowing, but rather as one of the integral details of an entire cosmological structure. Given adequate time and space, one could make a strong case that most Southeast Asian monuments of the Indic period were designed, at least in part, as cosmological symbols, serving to redefine the boundaries of time and space and thereby relocate the social sphere.

Fortunately, we need not pursue an exhaustive analysis of Southeast Asian monuments to discover the extent of their interest in Indian cosmology. Surely the most commonplace evidence of Indianization is the adoption of an Indian system of time reckoning. Both monuments and inscriptions nearly always pay the most careful attention to their location in time and space, either by invoking or depicting some intricate Indian calendrical system. The significance of these calendars cannot be over-stated: they not only define the basic parameters of time and space, but also locate the user within this framework. A ruler who dates his inscription "in the month of Māgha, on the first day of the rising moon, in Icaka 804" has thereby located himself, his actions, and his realm in a particular cosmological framework, a particular cycle of history. Indian calendars were the products of the most advanced mathematical astronomy of their time, portraying a vision of a vast and orderly cosmos which was the foundation for the metaphysical speculations of Hindu and Buddhist thought. And it is this vision that we find reflected again and again in Southeast Asian monuments, writings, and art of the Indic period.

But we need not attribute an excessive interest in mathematical astronomy to Southeast Asian elites in order to discover the reasons for their enthusiastic construction of cosmological monuments and symbols. Both Buddhist and Hindu versions of this cosmology link it explicitly to a theory of the state, which provided a strong justification for royal authority and a clear model for social order. This is the theory of the analogy, or structural correspondence, between macrocosmos and microcosmos, the natural and social orders, respectively. The organization of the state was patterned on the order of the cosmos, with the ruler analogous to a supreme god. Cosmological symbols thus became symbols of the realm, locating the ruler at its center (which certainly helps to explain the addiction of Southeast Asian monarchs to the construction of such symbols). These symbols often took the form of capital cities laid out according to sacred geometry, "diagrammes magiques tracés sur le parchemin de la plaine."[12] As Heine-Geldern explained in an early article on "Conceptions of State and Kingship in Southeast Asia,"

> as the universe, according to Brahman and Buddhist ideas, centers
> around Mount Meru, so that smaller universe, the empire, was bound
> to have a Mount Meru in the center of its capital which would be if
> not the country's geographical, at least its magic center.[13]

Or, as explained by a stele of the eleventh-century Khmer king Udayadityavarman II, "because he was aware that the center of the universe was distinguished by [Mount] Meru, he considered it appropriate that there should be a Meru in the center of his own capital."[14]

One of the most interesting examples of this architectural symbolism is the ninth century Khmer temple-city of Yasodharapura. This city was laid out around a central temple-mountain, oriented to the cardinal points. The central temple, the Bakhen, consisted of 7 terraces, representing the 7 heavens. There were 108 towers arranged symmetrically around a central tower, representing the 4 phases of the moon and the 27 lunar mansions

(4 × 27 = 108). From a point opposite the middle of any side of the temple, only 33 towers would be visible at one time, representing the abodes of the 33 gods of Indra's heaven. Similarly, 3 of the 5 central towers would be visible, symbolizing the heavenly cities of Brahma, Wiṣṇu, and Siva. From each of the 5 central terraces, 12 towers rose, representing the 12-year Brhaspati-cakra (Jupiter-cycle) which was used as a calendar from the fifth century A.D. onward. Thus, as Paul Wheatley observes,

> while in elevation the Bakhen was a plastic representation of Mount Meru, the axis of the universe, the kingdom and the capital, in plan it constituted an astronomical calendar in stone, depicting from each of the four cardinal directions the positions and paths of the planets in the great Indian conception of cyclic time.[15]

It was considered necessary two centuries later to undertake expensive modifications of the irrigation works around Angkor, so that it would resemble more closely the divine city of Sudarsana, capital of the god Indra.[16] Indeed, Angkor in the time of Jayavarman VII was undoubtedly the most spectacular example of the application of cosmo-magical symbolism to the human world. The main shrine, Angkor Wat, city of the gods, is the largest religious building in the world, a temple-mountain nearly a square mile in area enclosed by a moat 200 meters wide. The 9 pinnacles representing the points of the sacred cosmology were plated with gold. In the center was a golden statue representing the ruler as a divine incarnation, which was carried during festivals across the rainbow bridge that separated this celestial city from the world. Outside the capital, 300,000 people were servants of 20,000 Buddhist images in shrines throughout the realm. Feeding these people required 20,000 tons of rice annually.[17] In the words of Paul Wheatley, it was the intention of Jayavarman "to make of his kingdom one great offering to the gods of Mahāyāna Buddhism."[18]

Angkor clearly represented something of an apotheosis, but elsewhere in Southeast Asia one can find literally thousands of examples of the same cosmological symbolism applied to kingdoms great and small. Such symbolism linked the most sophisticated cosmology with a theory of absolute royal power, a blending of divine and royal authority expressed in cosmo-magical symbols. Here is ample reason for the interest of Southeast Asian elites in advanced Indian theories of the cosmos.

THE INDIANIZATION OF BALI

At about the time Suryavarman II was completing the construction of Angkor, a dynasty of princes calling themselves Warmadeva began the

Figure 2.1. Ninth century Central Javanese sculpture of the Hindu god Siwa, from the Prambanan temple complex, associated with conceptions of divine kingship. The style is purely Indian (Gupta). The sculpture dates from the same epoch as the earliest known Balinese Indic kingdoms and illustrates the Hindu ideals of godhood and divine kingship that may have served as models for early Balinese rulers.

construction of small stone tombs along a riverbank on the island of Bali. Ultimately, three rough tombs, each about ten meters in height, were chiselled out of the stone. Alongside these tombs, a monastery was cut into the cliffside to provide a home for the monks who would perform the rites of the cult of divine kingship. On a much less imposing scale than Angkor, the tombs of the Warmadevas were intended to perform essentially the same function: to identify the ruler with an Indic god and to suggest that the relationship of the ruler to his kingdom is analogous to that of the gods to the macrocosmos[19] (see Figure 2.1).

Remote from the great centers of Indic culture, small and historically quite insignificant, Bali provides us with a portrait of Indianization on a much simpler scale than Cambodia, Java, Pagan, or any of the other major Indic civilizations. But Bali became as deeply Indianized as any Southeast Asian society—worshipping Hindu/Buddhist deities with Sanskrit rituals, celebrating the great Hindu/Buddhist myths, measuring social behavior against the standards of an idealized version of the Varna ("caste") system. Moreover, "classical" Indic civilization survived on Bali until the twentieth century, long after the abandonment of Angkor and the destruction of the other great Indic states.

But the question of how and why Indian culture came to Bali has never been satisfactorily answered. In the author's opinion this is largely due to the fact that no one knew quite what to look for. Evidence of Indianization is abundant: over 250 Indic inscriptions have so far been discovered, covering a period from the ninth to the fourteenth centuries, and there are numerous archaeological remains, including sculptures, monuments, and ritual objects. But what seemed to be lacking was evidence of how these things came to appear in Bali. There was no evidence that Bali had been conquered or colonized by an Indian (or Southeast Asian Indic) kingdom. The inscriptions which began appearing in the ninth century suggest rather that indigenous Balinese rulers themselves adopted the mantle of Indic kinship and deliberately fostered various aspects of Indic culture, especially the growth of monasteries. One might be led to speculate on the successful conversion of a Balinese ruler to some Hindu or Buddhist sect, who then zealously promoted the new faith among his subjects, were it not that the inscriptions clearly reveal royal patronage for a multitude of sects. No single sect was given precedence; all were encouraged, suggesting that the ruler's enthusiasm for Indian culture went deeper than the doctrinal differences which divide sect from sect. Hence it appears that the Indianization of Bali was a voluntary—indeed enthusiastic—project of the Balinese themselves, that it consisted in the selective adoption of a broadly Indic worldview that involved a re-definition of the relationship of the social sphere to the cosmos, and that, therefore, Bali was Indianized by the power of Indian ideas—ideas given expression, for the most part, in works of art. If this is correct, then the question of how those ideas got to Bali—through the medium of traders, ambassadors, mendicant monks, or Balinese emissaries returning from a foreign court—becomes secondary. Perhaps one might add, "Fortunately!," because it is exceedingly unlikely that we will ever possess the evidence needed to settle the question of who actually came first. One suspects that in the course of time all of these possibilities were realized: monks, traders, diplomats, adventurers, and doubtless others came to Bali bringing news of the emerging Indic world and reflections of an Indic world view.

THE ARCHAEOLOGICAL PICTURE

The available archaeological evidence suggests that by the first millenium A.D., when the first evidence of Indianization appeared, Balinese society had reached the stage termed "Late Formative" (according to the standard comparative chronology of state formation originally developed by Steward).[20] In general terms, the Late Formative is characterized by social stratification (the rule of "chiefs"); advanced farming techniques, usually including irrigation; craft specialization and the development of long-distance trade; and the emergence of ceremonial centers. In Bali it is generally supposed that settled farming communities appeared as early as 5000–6000 B.C., with the arrival of Proto-Austronesian culture in the islands west of the Wallace Line.[21] However, there have as yet been no systematic excavations on Bali by which to date the development of early farming communities. But by the first millenium B.C., the Balinese became connected with a Bronze Age culture known as Dongson and identified archaeologically by the spread of bronze articles, particularly a characteristic large bronze kettle drum of which over 200 specimens have been found in Indochina and Indonesia.[22] In Bali a superb example of this kettle drum is preserved in a temple in Pejeng. Fragments of a casting-mold for such a drum were also found in Bali, proving that the Balinese of the first millenium B.C. were competent metalsmiths (using the lost-wax method of bronze casting). Along with the large drums, a variety of bronze tools and jewelry have been found in Bali. Many items of jewelry were recovered from ornate stone sarcophagi, suggesting the burial of chiefs and a marked social stratification.

The very earliest inscriptions found in Bali, dating from the late first millenium A.D., mention several implements used in wet-rice agriculture, including possible references to irrigation tunnel builders (*undagi aungan*). From these it has been inferred that wet-rice cultivation based on irrigation existed on Bali by the time of the formation of the first Indic kingdoms. Although archaeologists have not yet performed the research necessary to determine the sequence of agricultural innovation, it is generally believed that wet-rice irrigation developed well before state formation in Bali and Java. If this is correct, then the construction and maintenance of irrigation works must have been carried out by a Balinese society divided into chiefdoms and organized by ties of kinship. Further evidence of chieftainship is provided by numerous megalithic shrines, consisting of large open stone platforms surrounded by walls and containing upright megaliths.

Figure 2.2. Stone sarcophagi dating from the Neolithic period, shortly before the formation of the earliest Indic kingdoms. Along with human remains, they contained elaborate jewelry and weaponry, suggesting the burial of chiefs.

Similar megalithic temples are associated with many of the ancient chiefdoms of the Pacific, from the island of Nias, off Sumatra's west coast, to the large islands of Polynesia.[23] All of them consist essentially of open stone platforms with upright megaliths that served as homes for the gods and deified ancestors. Large sanctuaries such as those of Besakih, on the slopes of Bali's principal volcano, testify to the success of Balinese chiefs in mobilizing stonecarvers and laborers, who may also have been employed in the construction of irrigation systems. Thus by the late first millenium A.D., Balinese society was organized into sedentary villages ruled by chiefs. The major economic occupation was wet-rice agriculture, supported by small-scale irrigation. The economy supported craft specialists such as metalworkers who produced a variety of tools and ornaments. Long-distance trade was developing, and the Balinese were constructing elaborate megalithic ceremonial centers (see Figure 2.2).

The first clear indication of Indianization in Bali dates from around the ninth century A.D. and consists of three sorts of physical evidence: stone sculptures, clay seals and ritual objects, and a series of stone and copperplate inscriptions.[24] Both the seals and the sculptures are similar to those found in contemporary Indic Javanese kingdoms—the sculptures closely resemble those of Central Java, while the seals contain Mahāyāna formulas duplicated on Java in the eighth century temple Chandi Kalasan. However, it is important to note that these objects show no evidence of Javanese influence (whether conceptual or stylistic); they are obviously Indian and seem to have appeared in both Java and Bali at about the same time. Likewise, the inscriptions do not suggest that the Javanese played any significant role in the Indianization of Bali. Rather, they document the sustained efforts of indigenous Balinese rulers to restructure their society in light of the new Indic cosmologies and theories of the state.

Let us turn, then, to the inscriptions. The first of them were written in two languages: Sanskrit and Old Balinese. Inscriptions in Sanskrit proclaim the triumphs of early Balinese kings and are addressed to the (Indic) world at large. Such inscriptions are not unique to Bali, but are found throughout the western archipelago, and are generally interpreted as monuments intended to validate the status of rulers in the idiom of Indic kingship. Such validation was essential because of the cosmological significance of Hindu or Buddhist kingship. These inscriptions, chiselled into stone in a language entirely mysterious to all but a few Balinese, stand in sharp contrast to the inscriptions in Old Balinese. The latter consist of numerous lengthy texts in a Balinese language written for the most part on copper plates and addressed very specifically to particular villages or persons. It is in these inscriptions, I believe, that we can follow the process of Indianization. I emphasize the word process because (as we have seen) Indianization was not an isolated event—the arrival of the first monk, the conversion of the first chief, or the establishment of the first court—but a process that continued for many years and ultimately affected the entire society. (Even if, by some miracle, we were to discover the identity of the first "Indic" prince of Bali, we would still be left with the problem of explaining the subsequent Indianization of the whole society.) It is this process—the selective adoption of an Indic worldview leading to changes in the religion and social order of Bali, which were not restricted to the courts but spread into the villages—that is illuminated by the royal inscriptions.

The earliest known written inscription from Bali is Sukawana Al, dated Icaka 804 (881 A.D.). The edict is written in Old Balinese with Old Sanskrit (pre-Nagari) letters. It states that it was completed "at the law court at Singhamamdawa, in the month of Magha, on the first day of the waxing moon, the day of the market at Wijapura, in Icaka 804, and confirmed in court session." The edict begins:

> Know all you elders . . . my anxiety with regard to the hospice on the
> hill Cintamani mmal. There is no refuge for the people traveling in
> groups back and forth over the mountains.

That is the reason that orders have been given by me to senapati
Danda [a general named "Force"?], and Elder Marodaya, that a hermitage with a hospice is to be established in the [royal] hunting
grounds . . . .[25]

The edict goes on to establish the boundaries of the hospice and to create a
complex arrangement of taxes to be paid by the villagers in order to
provision the hospice with "earthen vats, sleeping mats and dinner things
for travelers who are overtaken by night on the road." Monks are
encouraged to reside in the hospice by exemption from a series of taxes.
Villagers are directed to help support the monks by providing specific
goods and services. Royal hermits are allocated a special, separate tax, and
villagers who die without heirs are required to give up most of their land
and goods to monasteries and hospices.[26]

Subsequent inscriptions make reference to a proliferating collection of
monasteries and "royal" courts and the gradual formation of a web of
relationships linking villages, courts, and monasteries. Inscriptions of the
tenth and eleventh centuries mention a wide variety of Hindu and
Buddhist sects, no one of which appears to have prevailed over the others.
Consider, for example, the eleventh century monarch Anak Wungcu.[27] In
his own inscriptions he is referred to as an incarnation of the Preserver of
the World, the god Wisnu, which suggests that he adhered to Vaisnavite
Hinduism. But his chief advisors included the heads of Buddhist and
Hindu monasteries, and he supported many royal hermits and sects (the
cults of Ganesha and Surya are specifically mentioned). Finally, the
inscriptions record his direct support of several large monastic communities, of which the remains of some are still visible in the hills around
Gunung Kawi.

The influence of the inhabitants of these monasteries was not
confined to the royal courts. An inscription of 1073 A.D. describes Balinese
society as being divided into the four castes of the Varna system
(Brahmana, Ksatriya, Waisya, and Sudra) and slaves (*hulun*). Regardless of
the degree to which society actually conformed to this model, the
inscription itself is significant as evidence of the ruler's desire to impose
Indic models on society at large, as well as on his court. Meanwhile, many
inscriptions record in great detail the varied ways in which villagers were
directed to help support the monks, including direct taxes, labor, and
defense. Monks might live in monasteries, at court, as hermits or
mendicants, or even in villages. But all of them relied on the villagers for
part or all of their support. From the time of the very earliest inscriptions
onward, villages were called upon to help support temples, monasteries,
roads, and waterworks, as in this inscription dated 975 A.D.:

[The people of the village of Jullah are responsible,] to the seawards, for the bathing place, fish-pond dikes, the earthworks, walls, dams, and warehouses [?]—seawards eastwards and westwards from there, for the distance of 127 fathoms. Moreover, if there is a weakening or collapse of the temples and cemetery, the waterworks, bathing place, tower-temple, or the main road—mountainwards and seawards—the villagers of Jullah, Indrapura, Buwandalem, Hiliran, all of them must take turns repairing them.[28]

The ruler also frequently directed the villagers to aid the hermitages in various ways, as in the above inscription, which continues:

Moreover, concerning the Saiwadharmman of the holy place there: the cost of bringing up stone must be paid in full by the village of Jullah. If the hermitage of Dharmakuta should be raided for plunder, everyone must come to the aid of the hermitage of Dharmakuta with weapons.[29]

Thus the villagers helped to support the temple and hermitages, and because of the practice of "tax farming" (direct tax collection by the ultimate recipients of the tax, rather than a specialized body of tax collectors), the royal hermits and holy men must have been in continual contact with the villagers, who served as their supporters and occasionally as their defenders!

Many of the royal proclamations are quite detailed, and from them it is possible to make some inferences about the organization of village life in early Balinese kingdoms, around the tenth century A.D. The evidence seems clear that originally the villages were governed by a body of "elders,"[30] as a kind of gerontocracy. Often royal proclamations were addressed very specifically to a governing body of village elders, who were mentioned by name.[31] This gerontocratic structure still exists today in a number of relatively remote villages—the "Bali Aga," which we will consider in detail in Chapter 6. In this connection, it is interesting that two distinct sets of terms are used in the inscriptions to refer to village institutions: Balinese terms, which are used to describe individuals, married couples, and the gerontocratic village hierarchy, and Sanskrit terms such as *kula, warga,* and *gotra,* which refer to descent groups in the idiom of caste. In some inscriptions, the head of a descent group (*kulapati*) is empowered to receive certain taxes.[32] Although it is not possible to learn very much about the nature of these descent groups from the inscriptions, the use of these Sanskrit terms is significant because it shows that Balinese rulers were imposing the terminology and conceptual framework of the Indic caste system on the villages. In Chapters 5 and 6, we will consider the opposing principles of caste and gerontocracy at work in various types of villages.

THE COURT-VILLAGE AXIS IN THE ARTS

Let us pause briefly to review the argument so far. To begin with, we saw that it may prove impossible to discover precisely when and how Indic influence reached Bali, because the archaeological evidence that survived to be discovered in the twentieth century cannot be presumed to be complete. But this issue is perhaps not so important as the question of the real nature of Indic influence on Balinese culture. As we saw, if one searches for the tangible objects that actually reached Bali from the Indic world, one finds no evidence for the arrival of armies or foreign officials, inventories of trade goods, or indeed anything very imposing in a material sense. What the archaeological record does show is the arrival of a great many complex *ideas*—caste, kingship, calendars, *dharma*, the "Three Worlds"—which we find very precisely articulated in written records, sculpture, and architecture. Cumulatively they appear to define a new vision of the nature of society and the universe—a new cosmology. Thus the most significant objects to reach Bali appear to have been Sanskrit texts, carried in the hands or the minds of persons capable of understanding and interpreting them. The grand theme of the Indianization of Bali and the birth of a new civilization must therefore be explored in terms of rather ephemeral events, such as poetry readings.

We are looking for the moments when a great civilization touched a small island, which we know resulted in the creation of a tiny but nonetheless quite spectacular civilization. Thus we are inclined to imagine a great procession of glorious Indian culture bearers winding its way across Java, over the mountains, and across the sea to Bali. A great priest steps forth, several heroes descend from Heaven, and in a magical moment Balinese civilization is born.

But what really happened, if the picture presented by the real archaeological evidence is at all accurate, was perhaps even more magical. The heroes, gods, priests—the entire procession—did indeed reach Bali, but it did so through the arts and the imagination. Embedded in the tax records and other prosaic sources, we find the record of their arrival: groups of artists who visited the courts and villages, conjuring the entire procession out of the air. The great procession of Indic culture bearers did not arrive once, physically, but innumerable times in countless courts and villages. It is quite possible, even likely, that not a single Indian visited Bali between the fifth and fifteenth centuries, when Bali's Indic civilization was coming into being. It is even more likely that no Balinese actually visited India. Indeed, the India that Indianized Bali—the India of Indra's heaven, of Rama's court of Ayudhya, of Mount Meru—could not be found by sailing across the Indian ocean.

If this analysis is correct, then clearly we must shift our attention away from the movements of men and goods and toward the movement of ideas, which as Lord Acton reminds us, "have a radiation and development, an ancestry and posterity of their own, in which men play the part of godfathers and godmothers more than that of legitimate parents." The archaeological record suggests two principal vehicles for the "radiation of ideas" from the courts and monasteries into the countryside: direct contacts of the sort we have seen illustrated by the royal inscriptions, and performances in which the arts brought to life the worlds of Indic cosmology. One might expect that it would be very difficult to find evidence for the role of the arts in villages a thousand years ago, but in fact the interest of the courts in village performances was such that quite a detailed picture is presented to us in the royal inscriptions. The very earliest inscription (the one that established a "refuge for people traveling over the mountains" of 882 A.D.) mentions a whole series of artists who are exempted from various taxes provided they reside in a designated village. In addition, both married and unmarried monks are encouraged by additional tax incentives to become villagers. These artists, monks and other villagers are instructed to create a hospice for "my pious people who may be overtaken by night on the road," who are to be provided with dinner and sleeping mats. Thus the very earliest Balinese inscription evokes a picture of artists and Hindu or Buddhist monks traveling under royal patronage, mingling with the villagers, and even becoming village residents. This picture is confirmed and elaborated in later inscriptions. For example, 14 years later a second inscription mentions a long list of artists who might "take refuge" in the village of Bebetin:[33]

> Also if there should take refuge and live there goldsmiths, blacksmiths, coppersmiths, *pamukul* [musicians], singers, *pabunjing* [musicians], drummers, flutists, *topeng* dancers, *wayang* [shadow puppet] performers, then their *tikasan* [a kind of tax] must be given to the Fire Temple.
> Bebetin AI (Goris 002)
> 2b.　4–5　896A.D.

In many of the earliest inscriptions, mention is made of the performing arts in the context of traveling royal performers (viz. the *agending i-haji*), who are empowered to support themselves by collecting fees in the name of the king for their performances in the villages. In somewhat later inscriptions, performing art groups based in villages are taxed at a low rate: so much per group, the amount varying according to whether the group is a singing, dancing, or playing (musical) group. The inscriptions show, then, that from the earliest moments in the history of Balinese civilization the arts were not exclusively based in either courts or villages, but flourished along an axis between them. Designated "royal performers" visited the villages regularly, and both monks and artists were encouraged to reside in the villages.

By the mid-eleventh century an intricate web of relations linked courts, villages, and monasteries. Monks and courtiers visited villages, village artists performed at court under the supervision of monks or royal ministers, and roving troupes of artists performed everywhere under royal patronage. Royal inscriptions distinguish for tax purposes three different sorts of performers: village-based groups, roving troupes, and royal performers ("singers who may sing before the king"). The full complexity of the system is evoked by inscriptions such as *Gurun Pai* (1071 A.D.).[34]

> Those singers, players, flutists to the limit of one in each dwelling shall pay *rot* tax as follows: singers two *ku*, flute players three *sa*, all to be offered to the god . . . .
>
> . . . And those who are *bhandagina* [entertainers] under the overseer in the *dharma* [religious foundation], those *agending angapakna ri haji* [singers who may sing before the king?] will be paid 2 *ku*; those *agending ambaran* [itinerant singers] will be paid 1 *ku* as *patulaka*; those flute players, *topeng* players, clowns, jesters, or players who perform before the king under the overseer, will be paid 1 *ku* as *patulaka*; the *anulin aqulu*, conch player, *abusya ta mulamula* under the overseer, will be paid 3 *sa* as *patulaka*. Those who request a performance to be provided for them at an unscheduled time must pay each player double . . . .
>
>

Gurun Pai, Epigraphia Balica I,
5a.   5   1071 A.D.

Patulaka is evidently the wage or tax payable: *ku* and *sa* are coins.

Here village artists performed at court under the supervision of the "overseer of the *dharma*," a religious official. The wording of the inscription suggests that such performances, and many others besides, were frequent occurrences. Thus by the eleventh century the court-village axis in the arts was in full flower, linking courts, monasteries, and villages together in a shared cosmological vision.

KINGS AND GODS

What was the nature of these "royal courts," which took such an interest in the welfare of monasteries and the affairs of village artists? So far we have merely described the courts as embodying, in some general way, "Indic conceptions of the state and kingship." But what were the actual Indic models for Balinese rulers?

Perhaps it is best to begin by saying what they were *not*. There is a considerable Sanskrit literature on the subject of statecraft, of which perhaps the most prominent example is the *Arthasāstra*, believed to have been written around 300 B.C. by one of the ministers of the great Indian Mauryan empire. The *Arthasāstra* is not precisely an account of the Mauryan empire, rather it is a general treatise on the science of *artha*, which has been rendered into English as "political economy" or "statecraft." Essentially, it is a handbook for princes, similar to Machiavelli's *Prince*, with which it is usually compared, in this and also in its rather chilling style. Cosmological and moral issues are entirely ignored, the only difficulties considered are practical: "From the helplessness of the villages and the exclusive preoccupation of men with their fields stems the growth of revenue for the royal treasury." Detailed models of administration are described: "Each eight hundred villages should have a major fort. There should be a capital city for every four hundred villages, a market town for every two hundred villages, and an urban cluster for every ten villages."[35]

Based on the inscriptions, it appears that by the tenth century there were numerous tiny "kingdoms" or principalities on Bali, each consisting of perhaps several dozen villages. By the yardstick proposed in the *Arthasāstra*, none of these "kingdoms" would have been sizable enough to merit a single market town! The entire island would have fit comfortably into a single district of the Mauryan state. Thus the details of real Indian administrative systems, as reflected in Arthasastric literature, could have very little application for the Balinese. In any case, Arthasastric manuals of statecraft are unknown in Bali.

The Indic models of kingship that the Balinese actually adopted derived from quite a different source: Sanskrit epics and religious poetry, which were carefully studied and eventually translated into a unique hybrid language now known as Old Javanese. From the ninth to the fourteenth centuries, Bali was closely linked to East Java, which developed a similar Hindu-Buddhist civilization. On both islands, the formal language of court poetry and administrative edicts was Old Javanese, which first appears on a Javanese temple inscription in 810 A.D. Sanskrit literature—in particular the great epics such as the Mahābhārata and the Rāmāyana—provided the model for Old Javanese literature, to the extent that much of the original Sanskrit vocabulary was retained intact—by one estimate, nearly 50 percent![36] By about 1100 A.D. this language replaced Old Balinese as the language of all Balinese royal inscriptions. Largely through the medium of Old Javanese, Indic philosophy and culture were made accessible to the Balinese and Javanese.

Old Javanese texts were of two types: *prasasti* (eulogies and royal charters) and *kakawin* (epic poetry). We have already examined some of the *prasasti*, royal charters commemorating the glory of a king or issuing laws and instructions to a village or monastary. The role of the *kakawin* (epic poems) in the life of the courts is perhaps best illustrated by an example such as the "Hariwangsa," composed in 1157 A.D.[37] The poem begins as its author, a court poet, is seated on a mountain-top meditating on the Hindu god Wiṣnu. He recalls that in an earlier age of the world, Wiṣnu had incarnated himself as the divine hero Krṣna and fought the great battles of the Bhāratayuddha. After the final victory, Wiṣnu returned to heaven. But now the world is once again threatened by evil beings and disorder. As the poet discovers, Wiṣnu has resolved to return to the Middle World of man as a world-conquering king. So begins the chronicle of the twelfth-century Javanese king called Jayabhaya ("World-Conqueror"), who is described in the poem as a living incarnation of the god: "Once universally known as Krṣna he has now incarnated himself once more as the protector of the world . . . ."[38] His battles are described in terms of the efforts of a god to restore world order. The entire poem is closely modelled on the Sanskrit epic Mahābhārata, with king Jayabhaya cast in the role of the divine Krṣna.

The model of kingship evoked in such texts is that of an absolute theocracy: the ruler is a god whose task is to maintain a cosmologically defined order within his realm. This thesis is proclaimed in royal edicts, eulogies, and epics such as the Hariwangsa. But clearly the degree to which such a claim is acceptable must depend very much on the success of its proclamation—particularly if there is more than one ruler aspiring to the mantle of "World-Conquering God." Thus the author of the "Hariwangsa" mentions his desire to help promote—through his words—"the invincibility of the king and the prosperity of the world." A court poet, like an eminent sage, stood in a special relationship to the ruler. Like the sage Agasthya, a poet understood the true nature of the ruler's divine mission: "Through the salutary influence of Agasthya's holiness and his superior knowledge of the art of governing, the dominant position of the king is firmly established throughout the world."[39] With the assistance of those who are enlightened and full of spiritual power, the power of the king is like "a fire fanned by the wind."[40]

Thus Old Javanese texts provided more than a readable blueprint for a cosmologically defined kingship. The texts themselves were magically powerful instruments which could help to realize the order which they described—vehicles both of enlightenment and of worldly power.[41] But to understand the nature of the relationship of these texts to the world leads us into another set of questions, which we must postpone for the moment (we will return to these questions in Chapter 4). It is easy to be seduced by the mysteries of cosmological kingship, but we must not lose sight of the fact that a world-conquering Balinese divine king probably held effective political control over a few square miles of ricefields and jungle.

What were the dimensions of an early Balinese kingdom? Based on what records we have, it appears probable that no single kingdom ever controlled the entire island. Instead, a cluster of tiny principalities vied for control of the rice terraces and trade emporiums along the northern and southern coasts. The early kingdoms of East Java, which came into being at about the same time, appear to have been considerably larger and more complex than neighboring Balinese principalities. In particular, East Javanese kings ruled through a regional administrative bureaucracy (*rakryan*) with the royal palace at its hub. In the tiny Balinese kingdoms, however, a regional bureaucracy was apparently unnecessary, and the courts ruled directly over each village. The nature of this relationship is nicely evoked by an inscription from North Bali, dated 1016 A.D.[42] On the sixth of September a delegation from the seacoast village of Jullah visited the court of Queen Sri Sangajnadewi to ask for relief from their tax burden. The village had been attacked by sea raiders several times, and many of the inhabitants had been captured or killed. Of 300 households, only 50 remained. "It is because they all became anxious about this that they paid homage to the queen, seeking the boon like a shower of *amrta* [Heavenly rain] that their taxes be reduced. Thus was their lamentation. The queen expressed her anxiety and compassion for the people of Jullah" and reduced some of their taxes.

The efforts of later Balinese rulers to establish their claims to rule were sometimes comical, sometimes rather terrifying. By the mid-eleventh century, a powerful Balinese dynasty called Varmadewa established control over much of the island and erected the stone tombs mentioned earlier. Adjacent to the royal tombs was the monastery, whose inhabitants carried out the rituals of the cult of royal divinity. In Java, rather more elaborate royal tombs (*chandi*) were constructed until the destruction of the Hindu courts in the fifteenth century. In Bali, however, the stone tombs were eventually replaced by more awesome symbols of divine splendor. In 1633 a Dutch emissary visited a Balinese court and described the events which followed the death of a prince.

> When a prince or princess of the royal family dies, their women or slaves run around the body, uttering cries . . . and all crazily solicit to die for their master or mistress. The king, on the following day, designates those of whom he makes choice. From that moment to the last of their lives, they are daily conducted at an early hour, each in her vehicle, to the sound of musical instruments . . . to perform their de-

votions, having wrapped their feet to white liniment, for it is no more permitted them to touch bare earth, because they are considered as consecrated.

[On the day of the cremation] the female slaves destined to accompany the dead went before, according to their ranks, those of the lowest rank taking the lead, each supported from behind by an old woman, and carried on a Badi, skillfully constructed of bamboos, and decked all over with flowers. There were placed before, a roasted pig, some rice, some betel, and other fruits, as an offering to their gods, and these unhappy victims of the most direful idolatry are thus carried in triumph, to the sound of different instruments, to the place where they are to be in the sequel poignarded and consumed by fire . . . The women were already poignarded and the greater number of them in flames, before the dead body of the queen arrived, born on a superb Badi, of a pyramidal form, consisting of eleven steps, and supported by a number of persons proportioned to the rank of the deceased. At each side of the body were seated two women, one holding an umbrella, and the other a flapper of horse-hair, to drive away the insects. Two priests preceded the Badi, in vehicles of a particular form, each in one hand holding a cord attached to the Badi as if giving to understand that they led the deceased to heaven, and ringing in the other a little bell, while such a noise of gongs, tabours, flutes and other instruments, is made, that the whole ceremony has less the air of a funeral procession than of a joyous village festival. When the dead body had passed the funeral piles arranged in its route, it was placed upon its own, which was forthwith lighted, while the chair, couch & c. used by the deceased in her lifetime, were also burnt. The assistants then regaled themselves with a feast, while the musicians, without ces- sation, struck the ear with a tumultuous melody, not unpleasing.

At the funeral of the king's two sons a short time before, 42 women of the one, and 34 of the other, were poignarded and burnt . . . but on such occasions the princesses of royal blood themselves leap at once into the flames . . . because they would look upon themselves as dis- honored by anyone's laying hands on their persons.[43]

Similar spectacles were observed by John Crawford, an English visitor to Bali almost 200 years later, in 1815, who reported: "On the death of the reigning king, the whole of his wives and concubines sometimes to the number of a hundred, or a hundred and fifty, devote themselves to the flames." Here was a personal testimony by the king's own wives and family to their unshakable faith in his divinity. These were the pageants of what Clifford Geertz terms the "Balinese theater state," designed to dramatize the king's supernatural authority before an audience consisting of the entire kingdom. The sheer dramatic power of these spectacles can be felt in Crawford's description of the moment when three royal widows prepared for their deaths.

When the corpse of the prince was almost consumed, the three Belas
got ready; they glanced towards once another to convince themselves
that all was prepared, but it was not a glance of fear, but of impatience,
and it seemed to express a desire that they might all leap at the same
moment. When the door opened (they were on a high gilded platform
above the flames) each took her place on the plank, made three
Sembahs [reverences] by joining her hands above her head, and
one of the bystanders placed a small dove upon her head. When the
dove flies away the soul is considered to escape. They immediately
leaped down. There was no cry in leaping, no cry from the fire; they
must have suffocated at once . . . . During the whole time from the
burning of the prince to the leap of the victims, the air resounded with
the clangour of numerous bands of music, small cannon were dis-
charged and the soldiers had drawn up outside the fire and contributed
to the noise of firing off their muskets. There was not one of the 50,000
Balinese present who did not show a merry face . . . .[44]

In his recent analysis of Balinese states of the nineteenth century,
Clifford Geertz demonstrates that such spectacles came to dominate
political life.

The stupendous cremations, tooth filings, temple dedications, pilgrimages and blood sacrifices, mobilizing hundreds and even thousands
of people and great quantities of wealth, were not means to political
ends: they were the ends themselves, they were what the state was for.
Court ceremonialism was the driving force of court politics; and mass
ritual was not a device to shore up the state, but rather the state, even
in its final gasp, was a device for the enactment of mass ritual. Power
served pomp, not pomp power.[45]

But in stating this thesis thus forcefully, Geertz may have overlooked
part of its significance. If we adopt once again a comparative perspective, it
is noteworthy that the mass spectacles of Bali do not seem to have
developed in other Hindu-Buddhist states of Southeast Asia—certainly not
to the same degree! Geertz argues that "mass ritual was not a device to
shore up the state," but surely in a sense it had to be. Rituals such as the
royal cremations served to dramatize the divinity of the ruler, and thus to
validate the basis for the Balinese state. But among other Hindu-Buddhist
states, the divine power of the king was often expressed more tangibly.
Khmer rulers, for example, had the wherewithal to excavate artificial
lakes and change the course of rivers around their capital to bring it into
closer conformity with the ideal image of a celestial city. But Balinese
rulers—whose temporal power, as we shall see, appears to have steadily
diminished over the centuries—lacked the means to construct world-cities
like those of the Khmer, Tai, or Burmese. The reformation of the world

into a divine order was therefore accomplished by the Balinese not by altering the course of rivers, but imaginatively—and not the less effectively!

The Khmer king Jayavarman VII (1181–1218 A.D.) labored for years over the remodeling of the capital city of Yasodharapura, to bring it closer to the image of Indra's heaven. The ceremonial enclave was surrounded by an ornamental wall 10 miles long, which in turn was enclosed by a moat 100 meters wide. Temples and palaces were reconstructed, and the hydraulic system surrounding the city was rebuilt to reflect the cosmic order, with new canals and even artificial lakes.[46] But impressive as Yasodharapura and its sister cities must undoubtedly have been, they remained things of this earth, and have by now fallen into ruins. Cosmic cities are perhaps best constructed in the mind, rather than on the ground, since the ones built by the imagination will always be more perfect.

THE ROLE OF THE COURTS

Clearly, the princes of Bali were caught in the contradiction between the universal and absolutist claims of the ideology of divine kingship, and the reality of fragmentary, postage-stamp principalities. By the eighteenth century, the island was divided into between 7 and 11 "major" principalities, each measuring no more than 30 miles square, all incessantly warring upon one another. Even these principalities were themselves closer to legal fictions than genuine autonomous states, since each was usually made up of a collection of semiautonomous princedoms. Thus in a peace treaty of 1734 between the principalities of "Buleleng" and "Tabanan," 6 princes were signatories on the Tabanan side and 3 on the Buleleng. A later treaty listed 38 on each side! In 1808 the paramount lord of Badung offered to sign a pact with the Dutch in return for an agreement that he be recognized as "Emperor" (Susuhunan) of Bali.[47] The lord of Klungkung, whose line of descent was generally accepted as the most illustrious and ritually potent of all the princes of Bali, and who was thus ritually entitled to claim the "Imperial" title, in fact ruled one of the smallest and weakest states. Literally dozens of princes and princelings struggled to reconcile their pretensions to grandeur with a resource base consisting of a few hectares of ricelands and villages.

Under these circumstances, it is not surprising that there is no evidence that any of the later Balinese courts developed any administrative machinery other than that required for tax collection and an army, which might better be described as a palace guard. As we shall see in the next chapter, complex regional institutions did develop in Bali, in the form of temple networks, but these were almost entirely separate from the courts.

Figure 2.3. Princesses of the court of Sukawati standing at the entrance to their family temple, the "core line" temple of the former principality of Sukawati. Although much of the palace was destroyed, the royal temple network remains intact.

The temple system which regulated rice production and irrigation paid no attention to the boundaries between courts and operated independently. Balinese politics had little to do with actual governance. Its aim, as Clifford Geertz well said, was "to construct a state by constructing a king."[48] The "royal palace" or court was laid out architecturally in the form of a temple, with the lord occupying the symbolic center, the axis mundi. Court ladies played the rôles of princesses and heroines (see Figures 2.3, 2.4). From the great royal cremations on down to the daily rituals of the palace, the activities of the court were devoted to the effective display of the cosmo-magical symbolism of power. But to understand the reasons for the proliferation of courts, each of them engaged in attempting to establish itself as a world center, we must carefully distinguish the ideology of Indic kingship from the realities of court structure.

Much that is puzzling about these Balinese courts becomes intelligible if we think of them not only in the context of kingdoms like the Khmer, but also in terms of the types of social organization typical of the Indonesian island world. Although Geertz stresses the uniqueness of Balinese state structure, another interpretation is also possible: that Balinese political structure was the outcome of the wedding of the ideology of divine kingship to a social organization based essentially on the conical clan. Such an interpretation helps to explain the proliferation and fragmentation of courts and the failure of these tiny courts to develop an effective bureaucratic structure of the sort associated with all large states, including those of Indic Southeast Asia.

Conical clans, a form of "tribal" organization common in the Malayo-Polynesian world, are based on a hierarchy of descent. "The chiefly lineage ruled by virtue of its genealogical connections with divinity: the chiefs were succeeded by first sons, who carried 'in the blood' the attributes of leadership."[49] In Kirchhoff's classic analysis, the line of chief's sons and their close relatives formed a core group termed *aristoi*.

Figure 2.4. Images of court ladies from a fourteenth century temple (Chandi Kalasan, East Java).

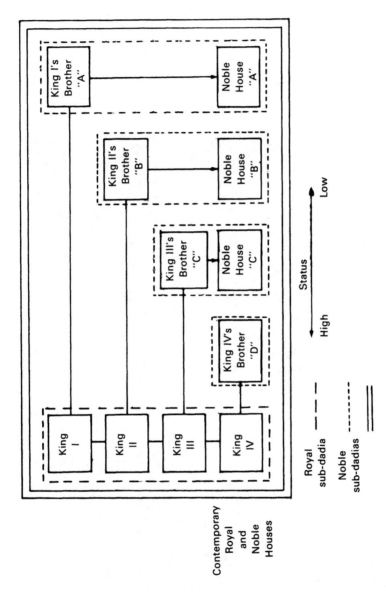

Figure 2.5. Gentry descent: the principle of sinking status. (Clifford Geertz, Negara: *The Theatre State of Nineteenth-Century Bali.* Copyright © 1980 by Princeton University Press. Fig. 2, p. 31, reprinted by permission of Princeton University Press.)

In societies of the conical clan type, it is regarded as a matter of course that all leading economic, social, religious functions are reserved to those of highest descent, i.e., those closest to the ancestor of the clan and tribe, who is frequently regarded as a god.[50]

Since one's social position depends upon one's closeness to the core line, endogamy is commonplace. As Kirchhoff notes, however, endogamy is "usually only for the *aristoi*. Marriage between relatives of high descent assures that their offspring will be of still higher descent. The type of preferential marriage most characteristic for this type of clan is that with parallel relatives; the brother's daughter or the father's brother's daughter."[51]

All of these attributes apply to Balinese courts. The "paramount lord," to adopt Geertz' terminology, owed his position to his birth: "Each upper-caste dadia (descent group) was considered to have a core line of eldest sons of eldest sons, stretching back in unbroken purity." But as Geertz explains:

As in each generation there were usually a number of younger sons of the paramount lord, there took place, over and above the perpetuation of the core line, the generation of a number of peripheral or cadet lines, each founded by one or another of these junior brothers. These lines, continued thenceforth by a primogenitural succession pattern of their own, formed separate dadias, but their status relative to that of the core line steadily and automatically declined as time passed.[52]

Among the nobility or *aristoi*, as Geertz himself notes, marriage was "preferentially endogamous, the most preferred marriage of all being with patri-parallel cousin (that is, for a male ego, his father's brother's daughter)," which helped to maintain the link of a prince to his "core line."[53] Thus in terms of their structure and internal dynamics, Balinese courts conformed to the general model of conical clans common to the Indo-Pacific region. The model of conical clanship helps in particular to explain the proliferation of rival courts and petty princes and the general framework of relations between courts, which were expressed in the idiom of kinship. This does not imply that Balinese courts were nothing more than conical clans, which is in truth to pose a false dichotomy, since the existence of conical clans in states (such as China) is well known. But it does suggest that the adoption of Indic models of divine kingship by the Balinese had the effect of consolidating a political structure prefigured in indigenous chiefdoms.

PUPUTAN (THE FINISH)

Classical Indic states survived on Bali until 1908, centuries after their disappearance elsewhere in Asia. The story of their ultimate demise is in many ways as revealing of the "imaginative energies" which drove them as the story of their birth. Moreover, the history of nineteenth century Bali is documented by European as well as Balinese sources. In the early nineteenth century, the island began to be visited by European traders, travelers, and colonial administrators in growing numbers. A Danish trader, Mads Lange, secured the position of agent for the Prince of Badung and established a prosperous trading factory on the south coast in 1836. Lange's establishment became a haven for visitors such as the scholars Friederich and Baron van Hoeval and the botanist Zollinger. From accounts written by such observers, as well as Balinese chronicles, we can form a picture of the classical courts as they approached their end.

By the nineteenth century, the monasteries that had flourished in an earlier epoch no longer existed—victims, perhaps, of the fragmentation of the political system. The nineteenth century political system was in Clifford Geertz's apt phrase an "acrobat's pyramid of 'kingdoms' of varying degrees of substantial autonomy and effective power."[54] The same scaling-down of symbolic pretentions to divine kingship that we observed in comparing early Balinese kings to their Khmer contemporaries is even more emphatically apparent in looking sidewise across nineteenth century Bali, where literally dozens of courts employed versions of the same cosmo-magical symbolism of authority. A minor prince could hardly expect his subjects to treat him as a living incarnation of Wiṣnu, but his authority nonetheless rested on his ability to claim some spark of divine fire as a son, grandson, or nephew of a *raja*, himself ultimately descended from the gods. At the top of the pyramid was the court of Klungkung, which traced its ancestry to the court of Gelgel, which in turn was founded by the lords of the great Javanese empire of Majapahit. Balinese chronicles trace the beginning of civilization with the conquest of Bali by Majapahit in the fourteenth century (although we now know that Majapahit was half a millenium too late to play the role of the great bearer of Indic culture). The royal house of Klungkung thus laid claim to the title of "innermost" (*dalem*) core line, and the *raja* himself was known by the title Dewa Agung ("Great God"). But by the nineteenth century the actual borders of Klungkung were never more than ten miles from the doorstep of the palace. It was not enough merely to lay claim to the title of sacred ruler, as is nicely illustrated by the story of a quarrel between the Dewa Agung and the neighboring prince of Gianyar, during which two opium dealers hung a straw effigy of the Dewa Agung in the public square in front of the court of Gianyar and invited passers-by to give it a kick![55]

Figure 2.6. One of the princes of North Bali.

Figure 2.7. Balinese warriors.

Throughout the nineteenth century, there was almost continuous warfare among dozens of courts and petty princes (see Figures 2.6 and 2.7). It has often been suggested that the princedoms of Bali "crumbled from the top down," that the conquest of Bali by the Dutch colonial empire merely administered the coup de grace to an archaic structure.

But despite the apparent fragility of the court system, the conquest of Bali required six military expeditions, beginning in 1846 and concluding in 1908. The wars began when Prince Jelantik of the North Balinese kingdom of Buleleng refused to acknowledge Dutch sovereignty, reportedly replying to a Dutch commissioner:

> Never while I live shall the state recognize the sovereignty of the
> Netherlands in the sense in which you interpret it. After my death the
> Radja may do as he chooses. Not by a mere scrap of paper shall any
> man become the master of another's lands. Rather let the *kris* decide.[56]

In response, the Dutch dispatched a force of 2 large frigates, 4 steamships, 4 brigs, 12 schooners, and 40 small craft, carrying 230 pieces of field artillery and 1,700 soldiers.[57] Buleleng was subjected to naval bombardment, then burned and pillaged.[58] The invading force then shelled and burned the palace of Singaraja. The Balinese princes eventually agreed to the Dutch terms: to demolish their fortifications, to build a fort for a Dutch garrision, accept a Dutch official representative, and pay the Dutch the costs of their military expedition! But when the Dutch fleet left, the Balinese refused to abide by any of these terms. Accordingly in 1848 a second Dutch fleet appeared off Buleleng, the largest military force ever assembled by the Dutch against a native power. But a large Balinese army under the command of Prince Jelantik was waiting for them behind extensive fortifications. After heavy bombardments, the Balinese gradually led the Dutch inland. By the afternoon of May 9, the Dutch had expended nearly 100,000 rounds of ammunition and were suffering from the heat. General van Wijck called for a retreat that turned into a rout. The Dutch soldiers abandoned their equipment and rushed back to their ships, pursued by Balinese warriors who challenged them to individual duels according to the traditions of Balinese warfare. The Dutch lost 264 dead and returned to Batavia.

The Third Expedition arrived off the coast of North Bali with the east monsoon in 1849—over 100 vessels, 5,000 troops, 400 pieces of field artillery, and 273 horses for cavalry. In a campaign that lasted months, there were few casualties until August 16, when a flanking attack captured the court of Djagaraga. Trapped in the palace, the wife of Prince Jelantik reportedly led the court ladies in a procession deliberately into the gunfire of the Dutch infantry. After the capture of Djagaraga, the Dutch com-

Figure 2.8. The Dutch cavalry regiment disembarks, September 12, 1906.

manders decided to sail to the other side of the island to attack Klungkung. Prince Jelantik was ambushed in the mountains and took poison. Hearing of these disasters, and of the Dutch landing in the south, the *raja* of the eastern princedom of Karangasem killed his wives, his children, and himself. Meanwhile, a force of 16,000 warriors from the South Balinese princedoms of Tabanan and Badung arrived to reinforce Klungkung, and the Dutch called off the campaign in return for acknowledgment of Dutch sovereignty. The Dutch in turn were bound not to occupy the kingdoms or interfere with internal affairs.

The Fourth and Fifth Expeditions were minor attempts to complete the pacification of the North. The Sixth Expedition appeared off the south coast on September 12, 1906 (see Figure 2.8). A Chinese ship had been wrecked on the reefs, and the princes refused to pay restitution to the owner, as demanded by the colonial power. Three battalions of infantry, two artillery batteries, and a cavalry detachment landed on the beaches of Sanur September 14 and marched inland. The high priest of the court of Kesiman killed his prince, who refused to lead a resistance. The Dutch

Figure 2.9. Dutch infantry before the gates of the palace.

Figure 2.10. The massacre of the court of Badung, 1906. The throne of the raja is visible in the foreground; Dutch infantry are on the left.

Figure 2.11. Balinese prisoners.

continued inland to the court of Badung (see Figure 2.9). As they approached the palace, the main gates opened and a silent procession emerged—the entire court, led by the *raja*, dressed in white cremation gowns with flowers in their hair and wearing their *krises* and jewelry. At a signal from the *raja*, the high priest plunged a sacred *kris* into his breast. The Dutch opened fire as the Balinese turned their swords upon themselves. According to eyewitnesses, court ladies disdainfully hurled their jewels at the soldiers, while Dutch artillery fired at the people and the palace behind. The palace was razed to the ground, and every member of the court died (see Figure 2.10). In the afternoon, the same scene was repeated at the court of Pemetjutan, although this time the palace itself was left standing. The army next advanced upon Tabanan, where the *raja* and crown prince elected to surrender and ask for terms (see Figure 2.11). However, the terms were not acceptable, and both killed themselves their first night in captivity, the prince with poison and the *raja* with an ornamental dagger in his throat.

Klungkung fell at last in 1908. The invasion began with a naval bombardment that destroyed much of the palace and the nearby ancient court of Gelgel. Once again, the *raja* elected Puputan—the Finish or Ending—rather than surrender. Dutch infantry supported by field artillery drew up 200 paces from the palace gate. The *raja* emerged at the head of his court, dressed in white, and walked to within 100 paces of the Dutch lines, where he plunged his *kris* into the ground. His high priest attempted to stab him, but both were struck by gunfire, and within minutes the entire court lay dead or dying.

CONCLUSION

The death of the Dewa Agung and his court marked the end, not only of Balinese resistance to the Dutch, but of the era of Indic kingdoms in Southeast Asia. The classical states of Bali were not merely conquered, but obliterated: the people killed, the libraries burned, the palaces reduced to rubble. It is all the more remarkable, then, that the cultural and institutional life of Bali—Balinese civilization, in fact—was able to survive. But as we have seen, the networks of court centers that constituted the Balinese "state" devoted most of their energies to imposing a particular image of order on the world. This image survived their destruction. The same myths that inspired the creation of the first kingdoms still fired the engines of politics in the nineteenth century, still compelled the social world to adapt to their visions of order. But to understand the evident power of these myths—the "imaginative energies" from which the state drew its force—we must look deeper than their manifestations in the spectacles of the "theater state." The real roots of this civilization lay elsewhere, in intertwining networks of thousands of temples where the power of the myths was guarded, nurtured, studied, and from time to time let loose in the world.

3
The Three Worlds

...the isle is full of noises
Sounds, and sweet airs that give delight and hurt not.
William Shakespeare
The Tempest

The present-day landscape of Bali is dotted with thousands of beautiful structures of stone and wood, which the Balinese call *pura*. The word *pura* is invariably translated as "temple," which captures their role as places of worship but obscures other features. In fact, *pura* are unique: they are quite unlike other Hindu or Buddhist temples, and play a role in organizing Balinese society that goes far beyond religion.

Elsewhere in Asia, temples are thought of as homes for the gods. But Balinese *pura* are empty most of the time; the gods are thought to be elsewhere. Temples are "activated" for only a few days each year by the arrival of the gods who are welcomed with a series of artistic performances. The entire artistic resources of the temple's congregation are mustered for days and nights of music, poetry, *wayang* (shadow puppetry), theater, and the presentation of gorgeous offerings. Then the gods depart, the remains are swept up, and the temple is abandoned for another year. This style of worship seems to fit the image of Bali as a society where religion is largely drowned in art.

But appearances are misleading. In fact, temples (*pura*) are the very backbone of the social order, forming the institutional structure of classical Balinese civilization. They are the means by which the process of social transformation, begun in the Balinese courts, was carried out into the countryside. Balinese temple festivals are much more than celebrations,

51

feasts of the gods; they are the occasions on which the many threads of the social world are woven together.

One way to approach the subject of *pura* would be to show how they organize different aspect of social life, from managing the irrigation systems to structuring village politics. But such an approach suggests that they are merely a deformed analogue or are equivalent to the institutions of Western society, religious institutions incongruously performing tasks of secular administration. Balinese *pura* make a great deal more sense within the context of the Balinese world view or cosmology. If Western societies have spent the last thousand years laboriously disentangling the secular from the religious, the Balinese have spent the same period attempting to integrate them.

Simply in the interests of clarity, then, it makes sense to approach the subject of temples from the perspective of Balinese cosmology. This is, as one might expect, an intricate subject, but even a simplified account can provide the groundwork from which the logic of temples can be seen. According to the Balinese, the world before our eyes is the realm of illusion, or *maya*. It is the middle World, between the Upper World of gods and the Lower World of demons. The gods are the forces of growth, while the demons are the powers of dissolution. It was by an agreement between these pure forces that the Middle World came into being as the realm of Life. The forces which shape life in the Middle World come from outside it and are ordinarily invisible—that is why the Middle World is the realm of *maya*.

In this tripartite universe, time does not move in a simple straight line, from past to present to future, but rather in cycles of growth and decay. The Middle World is the arena where many cycles of growth and decay mesh with one another to create life. This perspective on time is obviously very different from that of Western culture, where time is conceived of as linear, the present as a moving moment in a linear progression from past to future.

Recently, A. L. Becker suggested[1] that the Balinese cyclical theory of time, which has analogues in other tropical cultures from Cambodia to the Maya of Central America, may be related to the *experience* of time in regions near the Equator. In the Northern and Southern Hemispheres, the passage of time is clearly marked by seasonal changes: life begins in the spring, matures in the summer, and fades in the fall, beginning a new cycle the following year. But in tropical rain forests near the Equator, there are no pronounced seasons to synchronize the growth schedules of all living things. Instead, the processes of growth and decay proceed at different rates all over the forest, all the time. A flower is on a short, rapid growth cycle; a tree, much longer; a rock, longer still.

Figure 3.1. A *plintangan* calendar. For explanation see Figure 3.2.

Balinese calendars reflect this experience of time. Figure 3.1 shows a very simple calendar, designed to keep track of a five-day cycle intersecting a seven-day cycle. According to Balinese theory, each living being is on its own temporal/developmental cycle, a process of growth followed by decay. Events occur when cycles touch, when beings interact with one another in the Middle World. In this way, man and Nature are woven together: "The forest feels dejected in the month of Asadha, because its chill makes poets shiver and even sick from cold."[2]

The interaction of cycles gives time a kind of texture. The nearest analogue in Western culture may be the concept of "Friday the Thirteenth": when a Friday of the week cycle intersects the thirteenth day of the month cycle, that day has a special quality—dangerous or unlucky—determined by the conjunction of these two cycles. The calendar in Figure 3.2 depicts each of the 35 possible intersections of a five-day cycle with a seven-day cycle and shows pictorially the qualities possessed by each intersection. More complex Balinese calendars that keep track of more cycles, in terms of how they influence one another, are often made more

The Seven-day Week

Gods, wayang figures, trees, and birds

	Redite	Soma	Anggara	Buda	Wraspati	Sukra	Saniscara
Umanis	demon	palm	horse	weeping	broken axe	angry goose	floating head
Paing	elephant	incense	crab	elephantfish	false measure	fishtrap	arrow
Pon	suicide	message	dog	granary	cremation tower	broken *perahu*	flower
Wage	plough	ox	*perahu*	Pleiades	water pot	many debts	fighting quails
Kliwon	headless man	cart	boar	corpses for cremation	*naga*	lobster	urn for ashes

The Five-day Week

Buta (demons or elements) and animals

Figure 3.2. A *plintangan* calendar (intersection of five and seven day weeks). The calendar may begin anywhere, but is usually said to begin on Redite-Paing, the day of the elephant. The next day is the message, then the *perahu*, corpses for cremation, broken axe, fishtrap, and so on.

complete, for example, by adding the three-day cycle that governs, among other things, the market week. Which calendar to use, or which cycles to pay attention to, depends on one's purposes. The five-day and seven-day weeks are significant for many human activities, so this calendar is in common use. But someone planning an important or long-range project would be wise to consult a specialist in the management of time, who keeps track of many cycles, in order to try to keep the project in harmony with long-range cycles.

This brings us back to the subject of temples. A Balinese temple is best understood as a place where several cycles periodically coincide—cycles that connect the Upper, Middle, and Lower worlds. Many of the most powerful forces at work in the Middle World originate outside it. For life to continue in the Middle World, these forces must be accommodated.

The purposes of each temple "festival" (*odalan*) is to achieve such an accommodation. Gods, demons, men and women, and ancestors all have their own desires, and each has a role to play in the growing of rice, the prosperity of a village, or the continuity of a descent group. Temples are the places where all of the forces at work in some social sphere, such as a village, are brought together, so that each may be accommodated and that the institution or activity represented by the temple can survive and prosper for another cycle of its existence. Such compromises are never permanent and must be renewed each time the cycles of existence of all the parties involved (gods, demons, farmers, etc.) bring them back to the temple. When the festival ends, if it is successful, a compromise has been achieved and the temple grounds are emptied, the temple itself deserted until the date on which it must end this cycle and begin another (see Figure 3.3).

Consequently, the congregations of each temple are exclusively composed of the people who participate in the institution that the temple symbolizes. Every temple represents a social unit; it is a permanent institution, and only those directly involved in the life of that institution need to pay any attention to it. A second consequence is that people must belong to more than one temple. A person usually belongs to perhaps five or six different temples, each having to do with a different institutional system, from village administration to rice agriculture.[3]

Temples, then, are more than places of worship and more than symbols of social units. In an important sense, they are the institutional framework of Balinese society—the places where all of the forces at work in the life of an institution hold periodic stockholders' meetings. Since some of these forces are normally invisible, temples are also places where the veil of illusion (*maya*) that separates the Middle World from the other worlds is briefly penetrated, and invisible forces can become visible.

Figure 3.3. A 420-day festival in a village temple (Pura Desa). The young women in procession are bearing offerings and shrines containing spirits of their ancestors.

A typical "village" will contain perhaps 10 to 50 temples of this sort, not counting the small shrines to the gods and ancestors found in every houseyard. Some of these temples will pertain to local groups exclusively, but others will be linked to more temples elsewhere, thus connecting groups in the village with social networks that extend over wide areas, even across the whole of Bali. These are the permanent institutions of Balinese civilization, the civilization of the Middle World. Every institution must have a temple in order to function. Groups which do not possess a temple are called *sekehe*, from the Balinese word for "one" or "unity." *Sekehe* is a generic term for any social group that lacks the permanence of structure and purpose that would necessitate having a temple—a temporary organization, rather than an institution.

The dividing line between groups that ought to have temples and those that need not is based on whether the group's activities concern the group alone or must be made to coincide with the larger forces at work in the Three Worlds. In twentieth-century Bali, all of the major modern institutions—banks, the university, the post office—have built temples that hold festivals marking the date of the "activation" or beginning of the institution's life.

These remarks on the general definition of temples may be clarified by an example. Anticipating that some readers may be inclined to wonder whether these ideas about time cycles or a "Middle World" may be somewhat removed from the material realities of social life, perhaps it would be best to begin with the role of temples in organizing rice production. This subject takes us to the heart of village life, for irrigated rice terraces have been the economic mainstay of most Balinese villages for over a thousand years. Moreover, a glance at the endpaper map shows that the wet-rice heartlands were also the centers of court culture. As we shall see, the success of this system of agriculture depends on careful attention paid to cycles of growth and decay, as expressed in the idiom of calendrical temple rituals.

THE BALINESE WET-RICE ECOSYSTEM

The success of Balinese rice cultivation depends upon precise control of water. Cultivation begins with the flooding of the fields, which remain under water for most of the 105-day growing cycle. Gradually, the depth of water is decreased, until by harvest time the fields are quite dry. For at least a month after the harvest, the fields are left dry and wild grasses are permitted to grow. A new cycle begins when the grasses are ploughed over and the fields flooded. This alternation of wet and dry phases induces a cycle of anaerobic and aerobic conditions in the soil.[4] The activity of microorganisms in the soil varies with the phases of the cycle, satisfying the changing nutrient requirements of the rice plants as they grow. When the fields are flooded, blue-green algae form in the water, supplying almost all the nitrogen required by the rice.[5] Mineral nutrients are supplied primarily in the form of dissolved minerals in the water. The water excludes many wild plants that would otherwise compete with the rice for nutrients and sunlight, especially in the early growing phases.

The grasses that appear after each harvest develop deep roots, reaching nutrients that have been leached out of the topsoil. When the field is ploughed, the grasses are turned over, and as they decompose the nutrients are made available to the next rice crop.[6]

The same pattern of wet and dry phases that governs the development of rice in the four-month growing cycle also maintains the long-term equilibrium of the ecosystem. A thick soil horizon develops about 30 centimeters below the surface of the soil, which improves the water-holding capacity of the field and also traps nutrients that would otherwise be leached into the subsoil.[7] The stability of the ecosystem depends not simply on the availability of water, but rather on a carefully orchestrated alternation of wet and dry sequences for each field. Since there are no pronounced climatic seasons, it is possible to plant at any time during the year. Optimum productivity is achieved by staggering growing cycles along a watercourse so that some fields are wet while others are dry, and a relatively constant amount of water is required by the total system throughout the year.

This staggering of schedules is accomplished by an intricate network of temples, which coordinate farming activities from the level of a handful of farmers with adjacent land, to whole regions, and occasionally half or more of the island. Simplifying somewhat, the system works this way:

A group of farmers whose lands are watered by a common canal form a *tempek* (the name refers both to the association of farmers and to their lands), which elects a head (*klian*) and cooperates on work activities and rituals. The members of each *tempek* plant their crops at the same time and perform the rituals of the "rice cult" together at a small shrine in their fields. All of the *tempeks* whose waters flow from a common dam form a larger unit, called a *subak*, with an average area of about 80 hectares. *Subaks* tend to be larger downstream, where more land is available for terracing. Each *subak* possesses two temples: one near the *subak* dam and another in the rice fields. The ritual calendar of these temples coordinates the schedule of planting and harvesting for all of the *tempeks*, so that everyone plants at regular intervals (see Figure 3.4).

In order to ensure that not every *subak* follows the same schedule—and, in fact, to create an optimal arrangement for all of the *subaks* sharing a common water source—heads of *subaks* make annual treks up to higher-level "mountain temples" (Pura Masceti), to which dozens of *subaks* belong. At the festivals of these temples, *subak* leaders determine the ritual cycles for *subak* temples lying along the watercourse, and so stagger the planting schedules and water use for whole districts. Finally, two lake temples located near the center of the island coordinate farming activities for the whole island. A temple priest summed up the arrangement simply: "The local temples are children, offspring of the mountain temples. The mountain temples themselves are the children of the lake temple." Delegations from the *subak* temples perform the festivals of the mountain temples, and delegations from the mountain temples visit the lake temple once every 210-day "year" to celebrate the temple's festival and make decisions affecting subsidiary temples. There are two lake temples, Pura Batu Kau in the district of Tabanan, holding jurisdiction over western Bali, and Pura Ulun Danau, which is the "master water temple" for North, South, and East Bali.

This system is attested to in many historical records, including a report by a sixteenth century Dutch visitor. In late March of 1979, I found small shrines at the corners of rice fields everywhere in South Bali, erected for a period of 15 days in order to combat a prophesied plague of mice. Inside each shrine was an identical *mantra* and a drawing of a snake, whose spirit was asked to attack the rodents. The decision to erect these shrines was

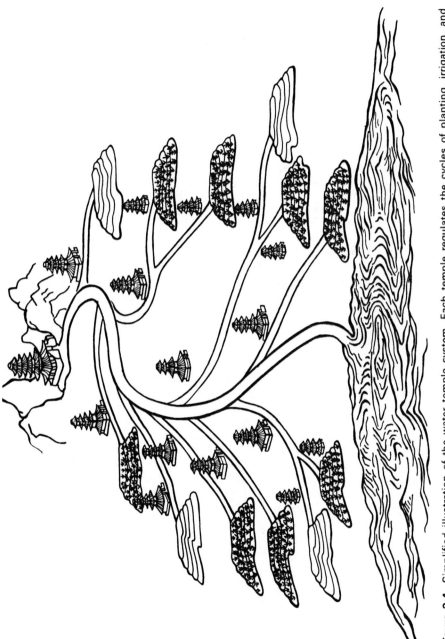

Figure 3.4. Simplified illustration of the water temple system. Each temple regulates the cycles of planting, irrigation, and harvesting in the fields around it. Temple cycles interlock to coordinate water use for whole regions, pegged to the ritual calendars of "master water temples."

made at the master temple of Ulun Danau and passed down via the network of temples and temple priests to all the farmers.

The delicate ecological balance achieved by the water temple system was underlined recently by several ill-fated attempts to abandon the system in several districts in South Bali. Following the advice of modernizing experts, farmers abandoned the ritual scheduling of activities and planted as often as possible, using fertilizer and insecticides to increase productivity. A steady diet of rice became available to predators such as rodents and insects, whose numbers were kept down in the old system by the regular district-wide breaks in planting, when the fields were left fallow. Soil conditions changed, fields became harder to plough, irrigation became haphazard, and productivity declined. By 1979, nearly all the farmers involved had returned to the system of scheduling planting by temple calendars.

WATER TEMPLE RITUALS

The nature of the ceremonies held in the water temples varies from district to district. F. A. Liefrinck describes a series of five rituals for northern Balinese fields in the late nineteenth century, while Clifford Geertz describes nine stages in the ritual cycle for the region of Tabanan:

> The nine stages were: (1) Water Opening; (2) Terrace Opening;
> (3) Planting; (4) Purifying the Water; (5) Feeding the Gods, a once-a-
> Balinese-month celebration in which holy water from the subak
> temple, the Pura Ulun Carik, was taken by each owner to his fields,
> and various food and flower offerings were made (as this ceremony
> was repeated every thirty-five days though the whole cultivation cycle,
> it was perhaps not properly a separate stage); (6) Budding of the Rice
> Plants (which occurs about a hundred days or so after planting); (7)
> Yellowing (that is, approaching fruition) of the Rice; (8) Harvest; (9)
> Placing the Harvested Rice in the Granary.[8]

This sequence of rituals to ensure the growth of the rice is often likened by the Balinese to the rituals performed for the human life cycle (called *manu sayadnya*). Farmers refer to the ceremony held when the seeds are developing as "when the rice is pregnant." When the seeds appear, a birth ritual is performed, which includes a marvelous performance known as "singing to the baby rice." Fields are purified after each major transition with offerings and holy water, just as human rites of passage are marked with purification rituals (see Lansing 1974, p. 87). Holy water plays a crucial role in these rituals and is a visible symbol of the links between temples that bind the whole system together. Holy water (*tirta*) is created by Brahmana priests from the waters of the central lakes, in ceremonies held within the lake temples, and is taken to the mountain temples, where it is used by other priests to make more holy water. Jars of this water are then taken to the *subak* temples, where still more holy water is produced by adding waters from the local stream to the holy water and then performing special rituals. Ultimately, this water is poured into the rice fields once a month, and the chain of rituals linking each farmer to the master temple is complete.

Water temples are linked to all other temple networks through the temples called Pura Balai Agung (Great Council Temples), which are found in every village. The gods from *all* of the temples in the vicinity of the village are invited, 25 days before the harvest, to descend into the shrines of the Balai Agung for a 3-day temple festival (*nunas sesari*). Processions stream into the temple bringing the shrines and accoutrements of many gods, the Rice Mother, and symbols of the crop. The assembled deities are entreated to endow the crop with succulence and strength-giving properties. In this way, the forces of growth are marshalled for the benefit of the harvest, which is essential to the general welfare.

After this comes the most important festival, the three-day "anniversary" festival of the subak temple, which marks the end of the cycle. A Dutch scholar, F. A. Liefrinck, wrote a beautiful description of such a festival held in 1886 in a temple in North Bali. It seems appropriate to end this account of water temples with Liefrinck's description, which begins with the temple itself,

> . . . a sanctuary set in the midst of the ricefields, with gigantic trees casting a cool shade over the high surrounding wall, the pyramidal gateways, and the shrines inside, so gracefully embellished with magnificent stone carvings.
>
> On the day preceding the opening of the actual festival, the *mekihis* ritual is performed. The members of the subak community, dressed in their finest clothes, carry down to the seashore the wooden caskets in which the gods are present and all the temple appurtenances, together with offerings of flowers and fruit. All of these objects are placed on the beach, then later, as evening begins, carried back to the temple again to the accompaniment of gamelan music. The ritual symbolizes the bathing of the gods who, thus refreshed, will be well disposed to accept the offerings to be presented the following day.
>
> The main offerings are prepared by the family of the temple priest, the pemanku, but every housewife in the subak community has been busy for days making simpler offerings for which the finest fruits and best flowers are used. Additional items required for the usaba (harvest) ceremonies and for the festival meals eaten at the temple—rice, meat, fruit, sweets, and so on—must be supplied by the members of the subak

in proportion to the area of their holdings, and in accordance with a permanent list stipulating which items each member has to contribute for this and other occasions.

Early on the opening day of the festival the members of the subak proceed to the temple, each wearing a waistband in which is fixed, instead of the more usual creese, a chopping knife enclosed in a decorated sheath. Seated on a long platform, they chop the meat which is to be cooked by the women. Next the rice is cooked, and at the same time the suckling pigs are roasted. The food is then divided into equal portions which are put on *dulangs* (wooden platters with pedestals), one for each of those entitled to participate in the meal. At several points in the temple gamelan orchestras play in turn, and the general festive atmosphere is heightened by dance performances.

It is the custom in some subaks that each tegakan (grouping of fields) must be represented by one *rejang*, a young girl not yet of marriageable age. Sometimes more than a hundred in number, these girls, elaborately dressed and wearing flowers in their hair, are led three times around the temple as they dance, the silver bracelets on their anklets tinkling to the accompaniment of gamelan music.

Towards midday the dance is over and the subak families make their way homewards, only to return soon after to the temple. This time the women carry on their heads *dulangs* piled high with offerings. It is not necessary for them to climb the high steps to the main entrance with their burden as they can enter the temple through a small side door. The offerings are placed on a platform in readiness for the evening ceremony. The men, enjoying a well-earned respite, collect for a few minutes in a gay crowd at the temple entrance where flower sellers are doing a brisk trade, and then, joined by their wives and children, they proceed to a stone structure facing the entrance. In this structure, decorated for the occasion with multi-colored strips of cloth, silk and paper sunshades, and ceremonial lances with peacock feathers, resides Dewi Aya Manik Galuh, the tutelary goddess of the fields and the crops.

The shrine is on a terrace where several *pemangkus* (temple priests), clad only in white, are seated on mats. Each family approaches with offerings which the priests, after mumbling a few prayers, accept on behalf of the goddess. The priests then sprinkle holy water over the kneeling doners and over the flowers that are distributed amongst the families.

The family groups next throng around dancers and other entertainers who are performing nearby in the temple enclosure. But there is not much time for these amusements because the farmers and their wives must hurry to their fields to present certain offerings. The women carry *jerimpens*, which are made of banana leaves, coconut-palm leaves, fruit and sweets, and are about twenty inches high. Following the women come the men bearing long bamboo poles with a cluster of leaves at the tip and with cloth wound round the upper part. The poles, with the jerimpens tied to them, are placed upright in the ricefields after some preliminary prayers and after being sprinkled with holy water brought from the temple. This offering is left in the fields.

Those who now wish to take part in the ritual in the temple at the river dam have to hurry back to the *subak* temple, for it is there that the procession is assembling to leave, as soon as the sun sets, for the river. Led by a gamelan orchestra and bearers of ceremonial lances, the participants carry offerings as well as shrines on platforms to the site of the ceremony, some two miles distant. At the dam temple offerings are presented with the same ritual as that at the subak temple. The ritual completed, the participants return home running and shouting, and are greeted no less noisily at the entrance to the village by those who remained behind.

Before long the boom of the *kulkul* drum resounds through the village announcing the resumption of the festivities, and soon the temple enclosure is thronged again with a happy crowd watching a dance of religious significance performed by young girls who, in this rôle, are called *sang hyang*. However, by ten o'clock many of the audience, particularly the children, are lying asleep either in the pavillion or in the open air to regain energy to be able to stay awake for the rest of the night.

At this point a group of the female temple servants fulfill an important task. While a *pemangku* shakes a tinkling bell, or *genta*, they sit on the ground in a half circle round the platform where the offerings to be presented on behalf of the whole *subak* community are guarded by temple officials. Breathing in the smoke that is rising in thick clouds from earthenware incense burners, the women gradually attain a state of hysterical excitement, monotonously repeating incantations as an invitation to the deity to descent so that the offerings can be presented. After the chanting has gone on for some time the temple officials stand up and, taking hold of the lances decorated with peacock feathers, they perform a brief dance that is intended to inform the deity that her devotees are ready to receive her. Usually the smoke of the incense and the drone of the chanting soon causes one of the women or one of the audience to twitch and gesture in a frenzy, wild-eyed and babbling incoherently. Soon the frenzy passes, and a clear voice announces that the deity has entered the body of the speaker.

The klian subak comes forward, presents the offerings and asks if the deity finds them acceptable. Having received an affirmative answer, the klian then requests that the coming harvest will be abundant, adding any other request the community may wish to make. The goddess also takes this opportunity to indicate which offerings must still be presented and the repairs and improvements that must be carried out in the various temples in the course of the coming year.

After this communion with the deity more incense is burned, the chant is resumed, and the gamelan orchestra plays a melody that is only performed when the *ngurek*, or creese dance, is to take place. Gradually more and more of the audience manifest a condition of excitement, unsheathing their creeses or seizing lances, and beginning to dance wildly, brandishing these weapons. The wild dance continues all through the night, a fantastic spectacle in the temple courtyard lit with no other light than the glow of the moon, obscured here and there by the high walls and the thick foliage of the trees. There may be as many as a hundred half-naked figures rushing furiously back and forward, repeatedly making motions of stabbing themselves and others. The klian desa (village head) is in front of the shouting mass, and from time to time he pours holy water or arak into the mouths of a group of kneeling dancers, who then resume their violent cavorting with new vigor....

The dance goes on until dawn, but as the sky becomes lighter the enthusiasm wanes, and the spectacle loses its allure. In the bright rays of the sun the ecstasy fades, the crowd thins out, returning home to rest, but again only briefly, for the festival continues throughout the day ahead. The members of the subak will participate in another dance, this time without ecstatic abandon. Later, the offerings of foodstuffs of which, it is assumed, the deities partake only of the invisible essence, or *sari*, are placed on the ground outside to be taken home by the owners....[9]

The festival ends with cockfights held just outside the temple gates, where blood is spilled to further placate the demonic forces invoked in the trance performances. Except for the "creese dance", which is now rather uncommon, the rituals that Liefrinck describes may be observed today in any one of hundreds of water temple festivals held each year. In the next chapter, we will investigate the nature of the performances held within the temples, but here it seems appropriate to close by summing up the more obvious "external" aspects of water temple festivals.

First, while other temples may hold their festivals according to one of several possible calendrical systems, water temples invariably hold their festivals at intervals of 105, 210, or 420 days. Most temples hold festivals on each of these anniversaries, with the grandest spectacle reserved for the 420 day festival. The reason for this schedule is surely the 105 day growing period of native Balinese rice.

Second, the purpose of the water temple rituals (including the ceremonies held in the village Balai Agung temple) is to accommodate all of the forces and deities which can affect the growth of the crop. Cycles of growth (the gods) and decay (the demons) must be made to mesh harmoniously each time a new harvest cycle begins.

Third, the local cycles (water use, growth, and human and divine activities) must be made to mesh with those of whole regions. This is accomplished by the rituals performed in the regional networks of water temples.

CONSTRUCTING THE MIDDLE WORLD

It is now possible to define more precisely the role of temples in Balinese civilization, or rather, to explain why they in fact constitute that civilization. Just as "water temples" effectively organize the cooperative aspects of wet-rice cultivation, so other temple networks organize the other major institutions of court politics, kinship, and village affairs. It seems plausible to claim that the use of temples as organizational systems was carried further in Bali than in any other Southeast Asian society, although in the Kandyan and Khmer kingdoms temples seem to have played an important economic and social role. However, there is no evidence that Khmer temples actually helped to organize production; their role seems rather to have been confined to the collection and redistribution of wealth. But in Bali, temples developed into complex institutional networks controlling everything from rice production to kinship. The development and spread of these temple networks was an historical process in which temples assumed greater significance as more and more aspects of social life were brought under their control.

This process—the extension of temple networks across the Balinese world—is more readily understandable in the light of another unique aspect of Balinese temples: their role as cosmological symbols. In Chapter 2 we reviewed the fundamental Indic conception of a structural correspondence between the order of society and the macrocosm. This idea found expression for the most part in the architecture of early royal tombs and capitals and in the symbolism of the four cardinal points, with Mount Meru at the center. Thus a Javanese royal tomb (*chandi*) or a Khmer temple mountain symbolizes the structure of both microcosm and macrocosm, i.e., the entire cosmology. A Balinese temple, on the other hand, does not represent a entire cosmology, but an integrated part of such a cosmology. No single temple represents the Middle World, but all of the temple networks collectively constitute the Middle World and define its relations with the other worlds (the macrocosm). This is obviously a very different image of the relationship of the social world to the cosmos. Temples are conceived as active links between the Three Worlds, not as symbols of a divine world. This points to yet another difference between Balinese temples and cosmological symbols such as *chandis* (temple mountains), or the vast cosmological cities of the Khmer. The latter rely primarily on architectural and sculptural symbolism to reflect the identity of macrocosm and microcosm, whereas for the Balinese, active linkages among the worlds are constructed imaginatively, through ritual and the arts. A dozen times each year, as the Balinese participate in the festival of the temples to which they belong, they are reminded that important human activities can never be truly secular because they occur in phases or cycles of growth and decline which do not ultimately begin or end in the human (Middle) world. Instead they lead into the other worlds. The linking of the Three Worlds is thus conceived of as an intricate, dynamic process.

Therefore, Balinese temples have a unique dual nature: they organize the affairs of daily life in a practical sense and at the same time reflect that life in the mirror of the cosmological concept of the Middle World. The ongoing cycles of Balinese temple festivals insistently frame the major activities of social life in a broad cosmological context, wherein temples themselves play a key role as mediators between the Worlds. In this way, a formidable feedback relationship is created between temples and performances held in temples. Temples exist for the purpose of holding festivals, in which artistic performances articulate the relationships among the Three Worlds, which in turn validate the existence of temples. If this is correct, then the spread of temple networks—there are now upwards of 20,000 temples on Bali!—is a consequence of the success of temple festivals in popularizing the concept of the Three Worlds, and hence the need for the temples. The *idea* of the human world as Middle World gradually became the *reality* of a society in which more and more aspects of social life were organized by temples.

This argument is strengthened by considering the distribution of temples and performing art groups across the Balinese landscape. Most of them are crowded into the oldest centers of Balinese civilization, which also happen to be the regions with the most elaborate networks of water temples and rice terraces. Using statistics compiled by each Balinese village for government records, we can form a rough picture of the contemporary distribution of temples and performing groups. Fortunately, the same statistical patterns emerge in each of the regions for which there are adequate data, so that the overall tendencies are quite clear. Bali is presently divided, for administrative purposes, into eight major regions (Kabupaten), the boundaries of which are based on those of the major Balinese principalities at the time of the Dutch conquest. Each region is further subdivided into from four to eight districts (*kecamatan*), which reflect the boundaries of minor princedoms. Thus modern statistical records pertain to the regional divisions which existed in precolonial Bali.

Figure 3.5 displays the relationship of temples (of all types) to the amount of wet-rice terraces (*sawah*) for a total of 16 districts in South and Central Bali (those which possess adequate statistical records).[10] The high

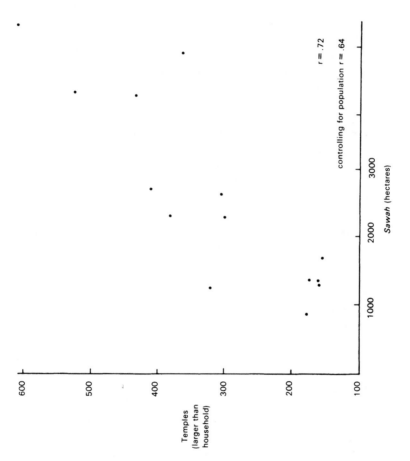

Figure 3.5. Relationship between the number of temples and the amount of *sawah* for 17 *Kecamatans* (districts) in Badung, Bengli, and Tabanan.

correlation coefficient of .72 indicates a very strong positive association between the number of temples and the amount of *sawah* in each district. This lends support to the thesis that Balinese civilization was furthest developed in the wet-rice heartlands. It was in the areas that *sawah* could be developed that the civilization of the Middle World came into being. As the civilization expanded, temples proliferated. But the spread of temples was not a simple function of population increase. Logically, sheer population growth does not lead to more temples, but to larger congregations in the existing temples. New temples reflect institutional changes, not demographic ones.

But does the high correlation merely reflect the fact that more people live in the wet-rice regions, so that the number of temples per capita is constant? Partial correlation analysis reveals that this is not the case, for the partial correlation of ricelands to temples controlling for the correlation of each population is .64, slightly less than the simple correlation of ricelands to temples, but still quite strong. The 16 districts chosen for this analysis vary in size from 36.2 to 406.1 square kilometers, and in population from 21,000 to 95,000, with a mean around 50,000.

A second interesting correlation is displayed in Figure 3.6, which shows the number of performing arts groups and temples in the same 17 districts. Here the pattern is even clearer. Performing art groups are *not* distributed evenly across the Balinese landscape, nor are they found primarily in the centers of population. Instead, they are closely associated with temples. The more temples that there are in a district, the more performing art groups. This strongly supports the theory that temples and performances are not really separate, but aspects of the same phenomenon. Temples exist only to hold performances; performances are held to "activate" temples. The more temples in a region, the more "activations," hence the greater the need for performances. Moreover, where there are many temples, the splendor of temple festivals generally increases as congregations compete with one another. Hildred and Clifford Geertz remarked on this tendency in the context of kinship temples: "The grander the group, the grander the temple; the grander the temple, the grander the ceremony; the grander the ceremony, the grander the group and so on, to aesthetic and liturgical heights which have astounded the world."[11]

Similarly strong correlations between temples and performing groups are found if we examine the independent records of each region, rather than aggregating them as in Figure 3.6. In Badung, the region with the most complete statistical records, the correlation of performing groups to temples is nearly perfect: .93 (controlling for population, .92). Again, it is reasonable to ask if this high correlation simply reflects the fact that some districts have larger overall populations and thus might be expected to have more artists and temples. But partial correlation analysis holding the

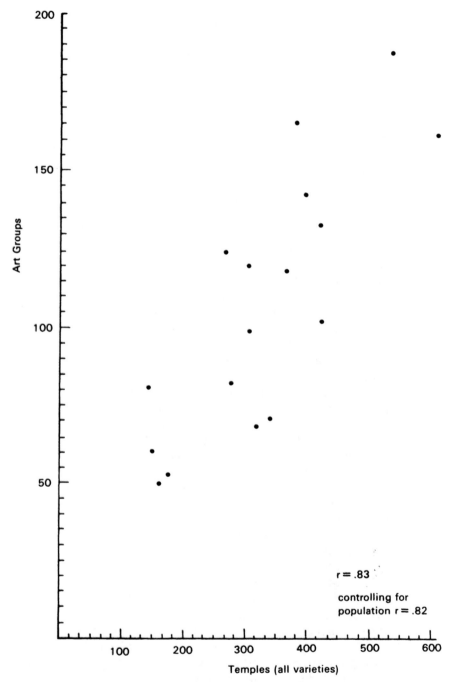

r = .83

controlling for
population r = .82

Figure 3.6. The relationship between temples and rice terraces for 17 districts in South Bali with average populations of 51,000.

population constant shows the same strong relationship, merely reducing the correlation for all 16 districts from .83 to .82.

The overall pattern of relationships is perhaps most conveniently displayed as a stochastic chain:

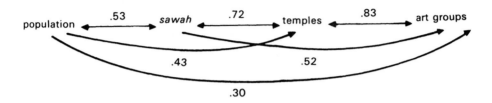

Each of the numbers represents the Pearson's r correlation between two variables. Plotted in this way, the entire pattern of intercorrelation among these four variables is visible as a strong Markov chain,[12] where each variable is most closely linked to the variables closest to it in the chain and the correlation weakens progressively to more distant variables.

What do these correlations show? We have already seen that there are substantial differences in the number of people, temples, performing groups, and wet-rice acreage in Balinese districts. The Markov chain shows that these differences are systematically related. The moderate correlation of population to rice fields reflects, according to my analysis, the shifts in population distribution which have occurred in the twentieth century as Bali's traditional economic system has been supplemented by new industries. My analysis would predict (actually "postdict") that population would have been much more strongly correlated with rice fields in the precolonial past. By filtering out the effects of the modern distribution of population, it is possible to consider the effects of *sawah*, temples, and art groups on each other more directly.

Sawah acreage is crucial to this analysis because the *sawah*-intensive areas were the heartlands of Balinese classical civilization. Indeed, this is shown by the strong correlation of *sawah* to temples. It was in the areas where *sawah* could be developed that the precolonial civilization of temples flourished. Today, temples are not clustered in the regions of modern population growth, but in the wet-rice heartland areas.

But what, precisely, is the relation of *sawah* to temples? As we have seen, temples are not a simple outcome of the logic of sawah production—if anything, the reverse is true, since it was the water temple system that organized the production schedules of the *sawahs*. It was the productivity of this total system which supported Balinese civilization. The temples were not a political or cultural artifact created by the economic system of rice agriculture; they were part of that system itself. Rice fields generated the wealth used to support temples and their festivals, while temples played a major role in organizing *sawah* production.

The strongest correlation is between the number of temples and the number of performing arts groups in each district, which supports the notion that temples are essentially theaters. Performing groups are only weakly correlated with population or *sawah*, which brings us to the last point about this stochastic model, that it can be read either synchronically or diachronically. Synchronically, it shows that performing groups in modern Bali are very strongly correlated with the number of nearby temples, and the number of temples is in turn related to the amount of rice fields nearby rather than the present distribution of population. Diachronically, it suggests that the spread of temples and art groups was not a planned development or the natural outcome of population growth, but rather a continuous process that occurred most rapidly in the areas of extensive wet-rice agriculture. *Sawah* then appears not as a determining factor, but as an enabling factor. If all this is correct, then it seems inescapable that the process of development of Balinese classical civilization is not yet over, since the temple networks continue to function and grow. The various manifestations of twentieth century bureaucratic civilization which have been introduced into Bali have displaced and rearranged the ancient civilization, without, so far, destroying it. The island is now home to the institutions of two civilizations so radically different that they manage to coexist.

Before proceeding further, it seems prudent to pause here to ask whether the kinds of statistical manipulations required for the stochastic analysis are truly legitimate. How much violence have we done to temples and art groups by comparing them in this way? Does it make sense to lump village temples with water temples, *gambuh* dancers with *gamelan* orchestras?

Admittedly there is great variation among Balinese temples in terms of their physical features, purposes, and the divine and human congregations associated with them, but the Balinese class them all as "temples" (*pura*). The chief defining characteristic of a *pura* is that it holds an "activation" or "festival" (*odalan*) according to a set schedule. *Odalans* are always occasions for artistic performances. The more temples in a region, the more *odalans*, and hence the more performances that must be held. Temples are the central focus for nearly all Balinese arts: artists and craftsmen are required to build, ornament, and maintain them, and they must perform their arts, make their offerings to celebrate their festivals, and read their poetry aloud within them. The statistics on "art groups" (above) refer to musical and performing groups, since plastic artists are seldom organized into associations. But outside of the courts, temples also provided the major source of patronage for architects, painters, and sculptors until the tourists began to arrive.

It seems worth repeating also that it is often considered to be more prestigious to invite art groups from different villages to perform at temple festivals than to employ the local groups. Thus some villages may be major patrons of the arts and yet contain few artists.

For many temples, the wherewithal to hold splendid festivals year after year is guaranteed by the institution of *laba pura*: tax-free lands owned by the temple itself, which may only be used for temple festivals and upkeep. The amount of *laba pura* varies, but for much of Bali it is considerable.

Temple Lands

Region (Kabupaten)	Sawah Temple Lands (hectares)	Percentage of all Sawah	Dry Temple Lands (hectares)	Percentage of all Dry Lands
Bangli	182	6	2923	11
Badung	396	2	827	4
Gianyar	453	3	714	5
Karangasem	291	4	5202	11
Tabanan	96	0	410	1
Klungkung	90	2	677	3
Totals	1510	2	10753	6

But *laba pura* is not the only resource used to support temple festivals. Usually, members of each temple congregation meet some weeks before the temple festival to decide on the scale of ceremony they can afford (from *utama*, maximal, to *nista*, minimal), and then assess themselves to bear the cost equally. If the temple owns *laba pura*, this is used first, and any remaining expenses are divided among the members. Sometimes part of the proceeds from *laba pura* are used to pay the temple priest. So the scale of ceremony performed for an *odalan* is determined by the total resources of the group and their willingness to spend them in this way.

It seems clear that the relationships between temples and art groups and *sawah* are not an artifact of statistical method but perfectly genuine. Temples are largely supported by rice terraces even now, and presumably the relationship of rice production to temples was even stronger in the past when rice agriculture was virtually the sole source of wealth. The relationship between temples and performing groups is even clearer: most of the expenses involved in temple festivals are for ornamental or performing arts. All temples hold festivals, so there is no reason not to aggregate the total number of temples in a district in order to see whether it is related to the total number of art groups in the same region.

CONCLUSION

The statistical analysis reveals a clear pattern of associations among performing art groups, temples, and rice terraces. Temples and art groups are almost perfectly correlated, and they are clustered in the areas where Indic civilization is oldest in Bali (if the archaeological picture is at all accurate), rather than in the areas of modern population growth. These are precisely the areas where the unique Balinese temple system achieved its greatest organizational triumph: an extraordinarily sensitive and effective technique for organizing wet-rice cultivation, which realized optimal productivity with minimal ecological disturbance. The functioning of these temples in turn depends upon their role in the cosmological system expressed by the concept of the "Three Worlds." For this reason, performances held in temples are vital to the successful functioning of the temple system. The relationship between these elements—temples, performances, and cosmology—is essentially circular: temples exist to hold performances, in which they are "activated" by the performing arts, whose function is to "sound the texts" of Indic cosmology, which establish a world view in which temples are essential to the continued functioning of the Middle World. It was these temple networks, rather than the "political" structure of the courts, which provided the basic institutional structure for Balinese civilization.

We began this chapter with the observation that it is something of an oversimplification to describe Balinese *pura* as "temples." *Pura* are wholistic institutions that integrate social, religious, and economic activities—functions which in Western society are generally kept discrete. Through the performances held in *pura*, the cosmological vision which originally reshaped the courts spread into the villages, gradually transforming the whole of Bali into the "Middle World."

Central to the functioning of *pura* is the concept of cyclical time and a multilayered universe. If the world of man were not a Middle World where other realities are hidden by the veil of *maya*, *pura* would be unnecessary. But given this cosmology, *pura* assume a transcendent importance as the places where beings and forces from many time-cycles come together, linking the Three Worlds. Not only in the performances held inside them, but by their very existence *pura* express the fundamental concepts of the Balinese Indic world view: the "unity of the cosmos, and the inter-relatedness of everything in it." Pura are empty courtyards, whose power to structure the world derives from the power of the "sounding of the texts."

4
The Sounding of the Texts

Homage to the god ... who is the essence of written letters ... concealed in the dust of the poet's pencil.

Sumanasāntaka

The oppositions between language and culture, speech and writing, *langue* and *parole* are the foundations of modern semiotics, the fruits of what Foucault has described as the "discovery of language" in the last two centuries in the West. They define the parameters of our discourse on language, a discourse based on our developing cultural awareness of language as more than a colorless medium of expression. Thus, for example, Paul Ricoeur investigates the nature of language by asking "What is a text?," a question which leads him to the oppositions between speaking and writing, and language and the world. For Ricoeur, the defining quality of a written text is precisely that it exists outside the world: "A text is somehow 'in the air,' outside of the world or without a world; by means of this obliteration of all relation to the world, every text is free to enter into relations with all the other texts which come to take the place of the circumstantial reality shown by living speech."[1] Speech, in other words, is physically present in the world—it occurs as an event in space and time—while texts hang in an unworldly suspension, awaiting a reader who may draw them into relationship with one another through the act of reading. Texts are in this sense timeless and detached from the world. Edward Said criticizes this view, but regards it nonetheless as pervading, indeed defining our modern approach to texts. In *Beginnings: Intention and Method*, Said wonders that "our interpretive worldly-wisdom has been applied, in a sense, to everything except ourselves; we are brilliant at deconstructing the mystifications of a text, at elucidating the blindness of a critical method, but we have seemed unable to apply these techniques to the very life of the texts in the world . . . ."[2] The subject of this chapter is the "life of texts in the world," a topic which, as Said observes, appears only on the distant horizons of the Western tradition, but is central for the Balinese and other literate cultures of Southeast Asia. Drawing upon both Tantric traditions of Art as a vehicle for enlightenment and more ancient traditions of animism and spirit possession, the Balinese privilege the "sounding" of the text as the foundation of a performative aesthetics. But the purpose of this chapter is not merely to show that the Balinese contrive to see the operations of speech, writing, and language differently than we do. We aspire, after all, to a general theory of aesthetics, a theory rich enough to accommodate the complex and interpenetrating relationships of art, language, and culture. But our studies—especially with regard to the role of texts—have so far been restricted to a narrow range: the significance of texts in Western cultures in the recent past. But texts are not always novels or advertisements; there is more to language than French or English; ours, in short, is not necessarily a privileged position. Therefore, the distinctions between speech and writing, poetry and performance, and language and the world, which seem to us to be a starting place for analysis, are not necessarily obligatory.

THE POWER OF THE SOUNDED WORD

In the Thai language, the word for text is *bot*. To interpret a text in a reading or performance is to *ti bot*: to "strike" the text, in the same sense that one "strikes" a musical gong to emit a note. Mattani Rutnin writes of Thai dancers interpreting a *bot*: "Those who can interpret the bot successfully, i.e., in terms of aesthetics, drama and emotion are said to *ti bot taek* [literally, smash the text to pieces—interpret the text with utmost refinement and depth]."[3] Thai aesthetics is therefore divisible into two branches:

1. The aesthetics of the text
2. The aesthetics of the sounding of the texts

The first is analogous to modern Western aesthetics in that it is a kind of iconographic analysis, concerned with questions of form, style, and composition. But the aesthetics of the sounding of the text is directed to the question of the ways a text becomes manifest in a reading or performance.

In the Thai view, these are quite different, if complementary, branches of aesthetics. We might sum up the differences thus: one set of questions is raised if we talk about a sonnet in terms of its intrinsic qualities, as though existing perpetually in some timeless Platonic realm of art. But very different questions suggest themselves if we consider the sonnet as it is performed, as an event occurring within a culture. There is a pervasive tradition in Southeast Asia which insists that the sounding of words or music has intrinsic power. This power is beautifully evoked in Shelly Errington's analysis of the role of prose stories (*hikayat*) in Malay culture.

> Hikayat were written, but they were written to be read aloud in a public place. As such, they are better considered notes for a performance than texts to be read in quiet solitude. People listened to, rather than read, hikayat. They were attracted into its realm through the voice of the narrator, which carried (membawa) and brought into being the hikayat.
>
> Not uncommonly, the reading of the hikayat is one of the events related in hikayat. Sejarah Melayu, for instance, tells of a hikayat being read when the Portuguese attacked Malaka. One particularly sinister passage in Hikayat Hang Tuah tells that Hang Jebat is asked by the raja to recite hikayat. His sweet, clear, melodious voice melts the hearts of listeners and renders them inexpressibly tender; the raja falls asleep on Hang Jebat's lap; and the palace women are inspired by lust and throw him betel nuts and perfume from behind the screen. The scene— or should we call it sound?—marks the beginning of Hang Jebat's treason. We hear of the power of words not only when hikayat are read. Words flow from Hang Tuah's mouth sweet as honey when he visits distant lands, and those around him feel love. The almost palpable physical imagery of the words flowing from his mouth points to their active presence in the world: they do not stand apart from the world, explaining it or representing it. They are a presence, having their effect in the world. Throughout the hikayat, the imagery of sounds and silence is pervasive. To *berdiam* is both to remain silent and do nothing. Of someone who is helpless the hikayat says, *tidak kata-kata lagi* ("he spoke no more"). Hang Tuah himself is wounded by the Portuguese near the end of the hikayat and falls overboard, to be retrieved quickly by his compatriots. The hikayat does not describe his wounds or the blood. Its significance falls upon us, rather, as we hear that for three days and three nights he cannot speak.[4]

The concept of "sounding of the texts" is based upon belief in the power of what Errington calls "formed sounds, whether of words in spells, or the reading of the sacred texts, or of gamelan music, or of the combination of music, voices and sounds in wayang (shadow play)." This belief in the power of "formed sounds" is widespread among Southeast

Asian peoples, and appears to be very ancient. Certainly it has an archaic flavor, suggesting a rather naive or even "primitive" belief in word magic.

But the impression of naiveté is shattered as soon as we confront even the earliest written texts. Consider, for example, the literature now known as "Old Javanese," which came into being in the Hindu/Buddhist courts of Java, beginning around the ninth century A.D. The first texts were poems, written in the tradition of Sanskrit literature, in a language which drew upon both Sanskrit and Javanese styles and vocabularies. Each poem begins with a *manggala*, an invocation that sets forth the poet's understanding of the relationship between himself, his text, and the world. The *manggala* begins by invoking one of many gods and goddesses, but

> it is not so much the identity of the god invoked as the manner of the invocation and the aspect in which the deity is viewed that matters. And these appear to be the same despite the variety of names. The god concerned is always the god who is present in everything that can be described as *langö*, the god of beauty in its widest sense. He is found in the beauty of the mountains and sea, in the pleasure-garden with its charms of trees and flowers and in the month when they are in full bloom, in feminine grace and charm. It goes without saying that he resides in the lover's complaint and in the description of nature, in the feeling that beauty arouses in the heart of the lover and of the poet. He resides in everything used for giving expression to that feeling, whether it is the spoken or written word, and therefore also in sounds and letters and even in the instruments of writing. He is the god of the board that is written on and the pencil that is written with, and of the dust that is sent whirling about, finally to settle, by sharpening the latter.[5]

The "Sumanasāntaka," for example, begins by invoking the god of "beauty" (*langö*), who is concealed in the dust of the pencil sharpened by the poet and is asked to descend into the letters of the poem as if they were his temple. This "god" is considered to be both imminent and transcendent, immaterial (*niskala*), and of a finer and subtler nature than the world, which is an object of the senses (*suksma*). It is through the apprehension of this god that one can pierce the veil of illusion (*maya*) to discover the nature of reality. This god, then, is both the ultimate foundation of all that exists and also its real essence—imperceptible because it is of a finer texture than the perceptible world, but nonetheless pervading everything "from the coarse to the fine" (*aganal alit*).

Obviously, the English words "god" and "beauty" are imperfect translations for the concept of such a being, essence, or experience. After a brave attempt at translation, Zoetmulder (the foremost student of Old

Javanese) throws up his hands with the remark that translators "must resign themselves to the fact that Old Javanese is exceptionally rich in this area of description, and has developed a variety of means of expressing [aesthetic emotion] which other languages simply do not possess." But Zoetmulder's remarks on the word *langö* (which I have been rendering as both beauty and aesthetic experience) are helpful.

> Langö means both "enraptured" and "enrapturing." It can be said of a beautiful view as well as of the person affected by its beauty. It has what we might call a "subjective" and an "objective" aspect, for there is a common element—the Indians would say: a common *rasa*—in both subject and object, which makes them connatural and fit to become one. Objectively langö is the quality by which an object appeals to the aesthetic sense.[6]

Thus in one passage of the "Sumanasāntaka," the waves of the sea are described as "a flight of crystal stairs down which the poet descends when, in old age, he ends his life by plunging into langö." The same theme of the way *langö* knits the essence of man and nature together, harmonizing the "Small" and "Great Worlds" (micro/macrocosm) is expressed in these lines from the poem quoted earlier, the "Sumanasāntaka:"

> When a woman wishes to die, she asks the gods to return her beauty to the month of Kartika, the loveliness of her hair to the rain-bearing clouds, the suppleness of her arms to the welas-arep creeper, her tears to the dew-drops suspended from the tip of a blade of grass.[7]

FROM LETTERS TO SOUNDS

The concept of *langö*—the subtle essence connecting the god present in the dust of the poet's pencil to the loveliness of a woman's hair or to the rain-bearing clouds—defines an aesthetic, and with it an attitude towards language. *Langö* can be pursued in two directions: inward, through the letters of the poem, into the deep interior of the poet's soul; or outward, into the world, through the sounding of the text. In the second instance, aesthetic questions focus on congruence between the text (its overt meaning): the sounding of the text (the ways in which it becomes manifest) and its effects on the inner and outer worlds. Old Javanese poems were composed according to distinct metrical patterns, of which over 200 are known to exist. It is clear that they were intended to be read aloud, and indeed such readings continue today among the "reading clubs" (*sekehe bebasan*) of Bali. These are actually performances in which the most careful attention is paid to both the sounds of the words and their meanings. A reader intones a line from the text, which may have to be repeated if he strays from the correct metrical pattern. Next, another reader will propose a spontaneous translation into modern colloquial Balinese. Once the "meaning" has been tacitly agreed on by all those present, the first reader chants the next line. The Balinese words for these "readings" (*mengidung, mekekawin*, etc.) are, I think, best rendered into English as "sounding" the texts, in both the sense of turning letters into sounds and of searching for their meanings. From this reading or sounding it is but a short step to performance, where all the devices of music, language, and the theater are employed to carry the meaning, the *langö*, into the world. Such performances are powerful—not because of word magic, but because the more beautiful (*langö*) a performance, the more attractive it will be. Sounding the texts dispels the illusions of ordinary consciousness and brings to light the underlying structures that bind man and nature, past and present, inner and outer. The events of everyday life are divested of their apparent uniqueness, and people become aware of themselves as acting in accordance with age-old scripts.

The sounding of the texts brings written order into the world, displaying the logos which lies beyond the illusions of mundane existence. Obviously, for this to be effective the stories told must bear an important resemblance to events in the lives of the hearers, or audience. Consequently, it is one of the distinguishing characteristics of serious Balinese drama, shadow theater (*wayang*), or other soundings of the texts that the performers must not decide on the story to be told until they have assessed the needs of the audience. Here is Wija, a Balinese shadow puppeteer, in an interview with an American storyteller, Diane Wolkstein:

> Wolkstein: How do you choose which story you will tell?
> Wija: It is always different. Before performance begins we are served coffee and tea by the community or the people who have asked for the *wayang*. I talk with the people. Very often those who have sponsored the *wayang* will ask for certain things to be stressed.
> Question: If you go to a village where there are troubles, do you try to solve them?
> Wija: Of course! That is my job! The *wayang* reflects our life . . . . Just as the Pandawas are always being tempted by the Kauravas, their enemies, we, too, are always being tempted by evil. By taking the shadows of the *wayang* into ourselves, we are strengthened by the struggle, and the victory of the Pandawas. The clashing of the swords and the heaving of the divine weapons is only the outer image of the internal battle.[8]

In essence, a *wayang* performance is analogous to that of a reading club—a sounding of the texts. Line by line, an ancient text is sounded, and then an attempt is made at translation and interpretation. In a reading club, this is done orally, while in a *wayang* performance music, puppets, and the theatrical skills of the puppeteer are used to enhance the interpretation. The whole performance is structured in such a way as to pose questions about the relationship of the text to those who see and hear it performed. The puppeteer is seated behind a cloth screen, which is illuminated by the flickering light of an oil lamp. Several hundred puppets are employed, representing the gods and heroes of Balinese mythology: inhabitants of the worlds which are ordinarily hidden from human sight by the veil of *maya* (illusion). The puppets are richly painted but appear on the audience's side of the screen only as dark shadows, suggesting that the reality of the gods is so brilliant as to be beyond human sight or imagination. The *wayang* screen is in one sense a window in *maya* that allows us to peer into the dazzling world of the gods (for whom *we* are monochromatic shadows). In special *wayang* performances held for the entertainment of the gods, without a human audience, the screen is not used. The stories must be evoked by puppets speaking accurate Old Javanese; the sounds of their voices, enhanced by music from the *wayang* orchestra, are intrinsically powerful. Thus, on the Mountain of Poets in East Java, a *wayang* performance goes on continuously, day and night, sometimes with an audience but often without one. The performance itself creates an order in the world, as in the story of the rampaging giant who was finally quieted by the sight of a *wayang*, which drew him in and made him cease his random destruction.

Before beginning a performance, a puppeteer ritually cleanses himself with holy water, holds the Tree of Life puppet to his forehead, closes his eyes, and calls the gods to their places. The puppeteer Wija explains:

> There can be no world without direction. The gods have names and
> places in the compass. By calling their names, they go to their places,
> their homes. The last is the east which is the place of birth, the
> beginning. At this moment, too, the orchestra is playing the sunrise
> melody. In the *wayang* the puppeteer is god, and he is asking to be
> located in his proper place—his center—so that the creation can begin.[9]

The gods whom he "calls to their places" have their homes equally at the ends of the world and within the self, according to Balinese belief. They are the gods of both the macro- and microcosm (in Balinese, "Great Realm," Buana Agung; and "Small Realm," Buana Alit). The structure of a *wayang* performance creates a rich and complex metaphor of inner and outer realities. The puppeteer constructs a world of pure illusion, which is paradoxically also the "real" world. Each audience—the gods and the humans—appears as a mere shadow to the other. The puppeteers animate the gods, who in another sense animate them. These are gods who rule the "Great Realm," yet are found within the puppeteers. These paradoxes of illusion and reality are fully exploited in the *wayang* and lead us deeper into the nature of the power Balinese attribute to sounding the texts.

Within the context of Western notions of the "life of texts in the world," it is easy to see that *wayang* might possess what we might call an "illuminative" function. A well-told tale in a *wayang* might "instruct" the Balinese audience in essentially the same way that a Biblical parable expounded in a church service is meant to edify a Christian congregation. But *wayang* performed without an audience, like the endless performance on Poetry Mountain, is more mysterious. The Balinese explanation for such performances is that wayang can *create* order, in both the inner and outer worlds. To create order in the world is the privilege of gods, but the gods themselves are animated shadows in the *wayang*, whom the puppeteers call to their places as the puppeteers assume the power of creation. It is significant that the effectiveness of *wayang* does not depend on the audience "really" believing that the puppeteers (or their puppets) are divine. In fact, quite the reverse is true, as the following example shows. One of the most popular texts for *wayang* is the tenth-century poem "Arjuna Wijaya." In this passage the god Indra, disguised as an elderly human, instructs the hero Arjuna.

> Blinded by the passions and the world of the senses, one fails to acquire knowledge of oneself. For it is as with the spectators of a puppet-performance: they are carried away, cry and are sad (because of what befalls their beloved hero or heroine), in the ignorance of their understanding. And this even though they know that it is merely carved leather that moves and speaks. That is the image of one whose desires are bound to the objects of the senses, and who refuses to understand that all appearances are only an illusion and a display of sorcery without any reality."[10]

Yet despite this emphatic disavowal of "magical" powers in the puppets, puppeteers are regarded by the Balinese as a kind of priest. However, they are priests whose aim is not to mystify with illusion, but rather to clarify the role of illusion in our perception of reality. As Wija explained: "Wayang means shadow, reflection. Wayang is used to reflect the gods to the people, and the people to themselves." *Wayang* reveals the power of language and the imagination to go beyond "illumination," to construct an order in the world which exists both in the mind and, potentially, in the outer world as well. The performance itself poses questions, in the minds of the audience, about the relations between imaginary worlds, perceptual worlds, and "real" worlds. In contemplating a *wayang*, one sees that the boundaries between inner and outer realities—imagined worlds, the world before our eyes, and the worlds of the past and present which we take to be "real"—are forever shifting and in flux.

LANGUAGE AND PERFORMANCE

It is characteristic of the sounding of the texts in Balinese performances that several different languages are used. Usually, they are juxtaposed—different characters speak in different languages—in order to exploit different properties of each language. Balinese libraries house texts in Sanskrit, Old Javanese, Middle Javanese, Balinese, and Indonesian. The first three of these are ancient languages, now spoken only in performances, where they conjure up the worlds of the gods and the splendid kingdoms of the dim past. In Alton Becker's useful phrase, they are languages used for "speaking the past."[11] To "speak the present," one uses Balinese or Indonesian. But spoken Balinese itself is divided into registers which carry distinct connotations of place: High Balinese is courtly language, Middle Balinese is formal speech between equals, Low Balinese is the vernacular of the villages. In the same way, the use of modern Indonesian invokes a modern urban context. As we will see in a moment, all of these languages and registers may be employed in a theatrical performance, allowing a single actor to step adroitly from one historical/linguistic context to another.

Realm	Language or Register
Modern world	Indonesian
Traditional villages	Low Balinese
Recent Balinese Courts	High Balinese
Medieval Javanese kingdoms	Middle Javanese
Heroic past	Old Javanese
Timeless realms of the gods	Sanskrit

In the following excerpt from the first few minutes of a "mask theater" (*topeng*) performance, a single dancer shifts from language to language (and realm to realm) as he tells the story of the invasion of an East Javanese kingdom by a fifteenth-century Balinese king, Jelantik.

Excerpt From *Jelantik Goes to Blambangan*[12]

Pensar kelihan, a clown/servant/storyteller, wearing a purple half-mask with round, bulging eyes, emerges from behind a curtain and begins to dance to the accompaniment of *gamelan* music.

Language	Speech
Middle Javanese (excerpt from poem "Kidung Tantri")	A story is told of the King of Patali, rich, proud, and full of dignity. (Dances proudly.) Truly magnificent! Proceeding now! AAaat! Ah! Ha, ha, ha! Arah! Hi, hi, hi!
Old Javanese (excerpt from the Old Javanese version of the Mahabharata: tenth century)	At dawn, the red sun rises. The rustling of leaves on the mountainside joins the sounds of the frogs large and small.
Middle Balinese	I'm so happy! So happy!. I never get bored, telling you about my happiness! Like today! Why don't I get bored, talking about my happiness? Ayah! Hi, hi, hi! Heh! Why am I so happy? Because I just now became a bachelor again! Hi, hi, hi!
High Balinese	Oh my lord and king, I try to follow you loyally. I beseech you, lay not your curse upon me, for I am going to tell your story now. *Singeh! Singeh!* Please! Please! I pay homage to the ancestors, to those who are already holy. And to the divine trinity, the Holy Lords Wiṣnu, Brahma, and Iswara. And I pay homage as well to all those who would make the countryside peaceful and prosperous here in ancient Bali. I ask for your blessings. I beseech you not to lay your curses upon me.
Middle Balinese	And why? Why do I offer up these prayers? Because, I am about to tell you of my Lord, the great King here in Gelgel, Klungkung, the great Dalem Waterrenggong.
Old Javanese (excerpt from the Old Javanese Ramayana)	Spinning round on his tail, the son of Subali rises higher and higher.
Low Balinese (the local dialect of Klungkung, where the performance is being held)	Aduh! What a chase those noblemen in the orchestra gave me! (He refers to the orchestra for this performance). Now I'm worn out! Already too tired to give you a show! Mind you, I don't mean to criticize. Not just yet! It's my first time here. My first time dancing with these musicians. Their first time playing with me. And I'm very old-fashioned. Just like an old

	dog. There's not much fur left on my hide and what there is of it is very short. Huh! Moving on!
High Balinese	My Lord and Master, Dalem Waturrenggong, is the ruler of this kingdom. His mind is troubled now, filled with thoughts of His Royal Highness, His Majesty, the King of Blambangan.
Middle Balinese	What could have broken up their old friendship?

In the space of a few minutes, the actor has invoked four languages, of which most of his audience will understand only two or three. He has quoted from both of the great Hindu epics, the Ramayana and the Mahābhārata, along with the Middle Javanese court poem "Kidung Tantri." He steps "out of character" for an instant to make fun of himself as a "mangy old dog of a performer," then instantly returns to his role of servant in a sixteenth century Balinese court. In a manner unknown to Western theater, he weaves the story into the world of the audience and creates connections among the many worlds conjured up by the languages and poetry he uses.

Ancestral visitation is an ancient tradition in Indonesian cultures and continues to play a part in many Balinese theatrical performances in the phenomenon called "trance." The spirit of a performer can be "inhabited" by the spirit of the one he portrays. In this sort of drama, the performer always enters from behind a drawn curtain, after first shaking the curtain in such a way as to suggest some Power taking possession of it. There is thus a certain ambiguity about the dramatic figures who emerge from behind the curtain: are they actors, or visiting spirits? John Emigh comments on the entrance of the evil king in a later episode of the performance quoted above:

> As the King of Blambangan shakes the curtain, thereby cueing a frenzied rush of percussive sound, he cries out in Old Javanese, "Behold, here I come, the King of Blambangan," and warns the audience that preparation is necessary to witness his powerful countenance. The curtain is yanked open and the king thrusts his animalistic hands forward, looking through the opened curtain into the performance oval, damanding to know whom it is he is facing. Is he talking to the warriors from Gelgel who have invaded his territory? Or is he speaking to the audience he sees revealed to him in a language which is no longer theirs? The ambiguity is deliberate. By shifting back and forth between the modes of illusion and visitation, the performer can playfully toy with the vantage point of the audience.[13]

The ability of different languages to evoke different "realms" is part of the reason why so many languages are employed in the theater. But from a Balinese perspective, differences between languages go deeper than their association with a particular time and place. Different languages are regarded as having different properties, and hence different constraints on their use. Sanskrit and Old Javanese, the languages used to "speak the past," are intrinsically powerful and may not be used lightly. The nature of this power has been investigated by several scholars, beginning with C. C. Berg, who drew attention to passages in Old Javanese texts such as the "Hariwangsa," which state the author's desire to promote, by the words of the text, "the invincibility of the king and the prosperity of the world." Following Berg, Zoetmulder observed that certain languages may create such effects because "there is a kind of identity between the word and what it stands for. But the degree of its effectiveness is dependent on various factors. It is high if the words are taken from a text or are borrowed from a language that is considered sacred."[14]

In modern semiology, this would be described as an iconic view of language. Michel Foucault has ascribed a similar view of language to sixteenth century Europe.

> In its original form, when it was given to men by God himself,
> language was an absolutely certain and transparent sign for things,
> because it resembled them. The names of things were lodged in the
> things they designated, just as strength is written in the body of the
> lion, regality in the eye of the eagle, just as the influence of the planets
> is marked upon the brows of men: by form of similitude. This
> transparency was destroyed at Babel as a punishment for men. Lan-
> guages became separated and incompatible with one another only
> insofar as they had previously lost this original resemblance to things
> that had been the prime reason for the existence of language.[15]

Thus according to Foucault, in the "classical" sixteenth century view, language lost its direct iconic nature at the Tower of Babel. For this reason, the oldest language (Hebrew), while no longer directly connected with the things it names, still contains "as if in the form of fragments, the marks of that original name-giving." This seems very close to the Balinese view that Sanskrit is close to being a "perfect" language in the sense that the connection between the word and what it signifies is not seen as arbitrary, but rather as intrinsic. Compare Foucault's example of this iconic view of language with Zoetmulder's:

> Foucault: Paracelsus asks "Tell me, then, why snakes in Helvetia,
> Algoria, Swedland understand the Greek words Osy, Osya, Osy .... In

what academies did they learn them, so that scarcely have they heard
the word than they immediately turn tail in order not to hear it again?
Scarcely do they hear the word, when, notwithstanding their nature
and their spirit, they remain immobile and poison no one."

Zoetmulder (quoting Old Javanese texts): "Whosoever listens de-
votely (tuhagana) to the story of Astika and the serpent-sacrifice has no
need to fear serpents."

For the Balinese, certain Sanskrit *slokas* possess this iconicity, and are
therefore "magical." Sanskrit is also supposed to be the oldest language.
More recent languages—Old Javanese, Middle Javanese, Balinese, and
Indonesian—are less and less iconic, but the power of Old and Middle
Javanese poetry resides in no small part in its iconicity, and for this reason
the manner of its sounding is critical for its efficacy.

Iconicity is dramatically portrayed as a possibility in texts such as the
Old Javanese Ramayana, in which powerful words spoken by a
character with sufficient *sakti* (power) *must* happen—which becomes an
important plot device. But it is not only the language in which the words
are spoken, but the circumstances of its utterance, that makes the words
come true. Sanskrit is most iconic—the meaning of a *mantra* cannot be
realized if it is not sounded correctly, in the proper circumstances. On the
other hand, words spoken in Indonesian or modern Balinese cannot be
iconic under any circumstances. Thus, it is only in the total context of a
performance that the issue of the relationship of a symbol to its referent
can be settled. For an articulate Balinese, language can seemingly take on
any resonance, from a sound which echoes music, and is the true name of
a thing, to words rich with archaic associations and social connotations, to
mere weightless, arbitrary signs.

This suggests an important difference between the Western and
Balinese attitudes toward the relationship of a particular languages to the
world. Foucault poses this question in an interesting way in the concept of
the *episteme*, the principles of linguistic order, or classification, that
establish preconditions for systems of knowledge. For Foucault there is no
order,

no similitude and no distinction, even for the wholly untrained
perception, that is not the result of a precise operation and of the
application of a preliminary criterion. A "system of elements"—a
definition of the segments by which those segments can be affected,
and lastly, the threshold above which there is a difference and below
which there is a similitude—is indispensable for the establishment of
even the simplest form of order.

In *The Order of Things*, Foucault examines, for Post-Medieval European culture "what modalities of order have been recognized, posited, linked with space and time, in order to create the positive basis of knowledge as we find it employed in grammar and philology, in natural history and biology, in the study of wealth and political economy."[16]

Foucault traces the succession of epistemes as a linear process in which one episteme succeeds another. Thus, in his view, "classical" thought crumbled at the end of the eighteenth century when language ceased utterly to be iconic, and "words wandered off on their own." Foucault shares with Derrida a perception that the "modernity" of our thought is based on our discovery of language, that is, our sense of language as the "empty play of signifiers." Foucault's perception of a linear succession of epistemes in Western culture, each ultimately grounded in a different linguistic order, provides a clear contrast to the relationship of language to culture in Bali. Here languages and textual traditions do not succeed one another; rather, they coexist and interact with one another. In the space of a few minutes, as we saw in the excerpt from *Jelantik Goes to Blambangan*, a Balinese actor can employ the different properties of several languages to construct, in the minds of the audience, several distinct "realms" or realities. It is precisely the juxtaposition of different realms—or in Foucault's terminology, epistemes—that create the drama. The plot of a "story" is secondary, almost unimportant. Theatrical tension is created by the interaction of the "imaginary" realms with the present situation of the audience. Because stories must not be chosen beforehand, the challenge for performers is to bring the different textual traditions of the past to bear on the novelties of the present, molding them into continuing patterns of order.

CLOWNS, MUSIC, AND THE BOUNDARIES OF TIME

We have seen that the different languages of Bali are each associated with a different realm, and that these realms are arranged in a sort of chronological order, from ancient times to the present. It has also been hinted that different languages are often associated with different musical styles, in the context of dramatic performances. This association of music with language may seem somewhat foreign to us, but from the standpoint of Balinese aesthetics, the sounding of words and music are intimately related. Music is never merely ornamental, it is an integral part of the process by which the boundaries between the worlds are made permeable. The sounds of powerful words are mingled with the flow of music, which has the power to shape and bend time itself, in the minds of the hearers. The flow of sounds creates a tempo, a perceived rhythm of time. Thus as the texts are sounded, performers and even members of the audience are caught up in the flow, experiencing sounds to which they fit their movements, their thoughts, and ultimately, perhaps, their whole perception. Obviously this is not only a Balinese phenomenon; it is the common human experience of music. But Balinese aesthetics emphasizes the power of music to shape people's perceptions, particularly of time and temporal rhythms. For the Balinese, absorption in the flow of sounds can finally be total, leading to the state of "trance" in which one is "in" the music-time or music-world. This is not simply a passive state of musical rapture, the absorption in the sounds alone that comes with listening attentively to a good performer. It is, or rather is described by the Balinese as being, an active experience of being *in* the music-world, other-world. This is possible because the sounds of the music and the text are iconic for one another, and both point to a particular imaginary world. The music-world *is* the place spoken of in the text and portrayed by the dancers or puppets. Watching a performance on an admittedly rather bare and tatty stage or *wayang* screen, one is nonetheless carried along by the flow of sounds to lose oneself amid the images of the myths.

As Judith Becker has recently shown, the flow of music is the basic metaphor in Balinese thought for the flow of time. The Balinese conceptualize time not in terms of a linear flow, but rather as many repeating cycles, which reflect the rhythms of growth in the natural world. Calendars depict the intersections of different cycles, or weeks. In a Balinese *gamelan* orchestra, each musician plays a cyclical, repetitive piece, and the fabric of the melody is created by the interlocking of the various cycles. Becker explains that "the fundamental governing principle in gamelan music is the cyclic recurrence of a melodic/temporal unit, which is a musical manifestation of the way in which the passage of time is also ordered."[17]

The intersection of cycles gives time, as well as music, a kind of texture. Each day has a meaning, a quality, according to where it falls in the intersection of several cycles. This concept is essentially foreign to Western calendars, although we do have a single example: Friday the Thirteenth, a special kind of day with a quality inherent in its position at the juncture of two cycles. By showing the qualities of different intersecting cycles, Balinese calendars tell, as Clifford Geertz put it, "not what time it is, but what *kind* of time it is."[18] These cycles are not arbitrary units, but are regarded as expressing the true rhythms of time. According to Balinese cosmology, every living being is on its own temporal or developmental cycle, a process of growth followed by decay. Events occur as cycles touch, when beings interact with one another in the "Middle World." In this way, past and present, man and nature, are not separated, but woven together: "The forest feels dejected in the month of Asadha, because its chill makes poets shiver and even sick from cold."

But in the theater there are special characters who alone are immune to the cycles of time, characters who move across the boundaries of time, music, and language. These characters are of special interest because they are not mentioned in any of the ancient texts but play an important part nonetheless in the telling of most stories. They are called *parekan*, a word usually translated into English as "clowns" or "fools," and they are indeed bumbling, odd-shaped, buffoonish creatures who play the role of servants to the gods and heroes of the stories. Their chief function appears to be one of translation: when it seems likely that members of the audience do not understand part of the story (probably because they do not understand the language being used, for few Balinese are fluent in all the languages of the theater), the clowns step in, translating and interpreting, making jokes, and rendering everything into Low Balinese.

The function of these clowns poses an interesting problem about the relationship of the text to the audience. In one sense, they bring the drama to the audience as helpful translators. But their function as translators could easily be obviated by translating the text itself, as we perform Aeschuylus in modern English. So the structural effect of retaining the clowns is really the reverse: to create a space between the world of the audience and the text as it is invoked on stage. The clowns create a liminal space for themselves and play with the structures that create the boundaries of the performance: music, language, and dramatic style. Mediating between performers and audience, they speak to themselves, to the audience, and to the mythical characters who speak the words of the ancient texts. Like all clowns, they have no social position and are therefore free to comment on the social dramas they observe. We might think of them as cousins to Shakespeare's fools—except that in Shakespeare, the clowns never speak directly to the audience, though they are forever trying to instill a reflexive awareness in their lords and masters, as the Fool does for Lear.

But what distinguishes Balinese clowns from those of the European tradition is their power of translation, the power to control the sounding of the texts. Dancing back and forth between performers and audience, translating and enhancing some words while allowing others to pass into the void, they create the channels for the sounding of the text. In this sense, they are the masters of poesis, the use of words to create poetic worlds which are more true and more real than the everyday waking world of the audience. That the Balinese recognize this power as supreme is shown in the worst-kept secret of the Balinese theater, the identity of the greatest of these clowns, Twalen. Twalen is the prince of fools, a fat Falstaffian buffoon who usually plays the servant of the godlike Pandavas. But in reality, as everyone knows, Twalen is the elder brother of Siwa, greatest of the gods, and is thus older and more powerful than all the gods.

CONCLUSION

One of the major trends in poststructuralist semiotics has been a progressive distancing of the author, and the reader, from the text. In part this derives from an early emphasis, in structural linguistics, on viewing languages as systems of signs, autonomous in the sense that they may be understood without reference to the minds of speaker or hearer, writer or reader. More recently, this view of language has been challenged. Chomsky argued that language must be understood in relation to mind, helping to inaugurate a poststructuralist phase in linguistics. Few linguists now see language from a strictly Saussurean perspective, as an "autonomous" system of signs.

Separation of language and mind has also been strongly challenged from an evolutionary, biological perspective. Increasingly, studies of the role of language in the brain suggest that language and thought are inextricably linked, and that the origin of human (as distinct from animal) language does not lie in social communication. For that purpose, according to most researchers, a much simpler language consisting of a few hundred signs would be ample. A. J. Jerison provides a persuasive summary of research on the evolution of symbolic language in the human line.

> If there were selection pressures toward the development of language specifically for communication, we would expect the evolutionary response to be the development of "prewired" language systems with conventional sounds and symbols. These are the typical approaches to communication in other vertebrates, and they are accomplished (as in birds) with little or no learning and with relatively small neural systems. The very flexibility and plasticity of the language systems of the human brain argue for their evolution as having been analogous to that of other sensory integrative systems, which are now known to be unusually plastic, or modifiable by early experience. [Benjamin Lee Whorf and Edward Sapir pointed this out many years ago as one of the maladaptive features of this flexibility of the language system, which enables different societies to develop different languages and hence different realities, often with catastrophic effects on the interactions of human communities.]
>
> I am proposing here that the role of language in communication first evolved as a side effect of its basic role in the perception of reality. The fact that communication is so central to our present view of language does not affect the argument. It is, in fact, theoretically elegant to explain the evolution of an important novel adaptation in a species by relating it to the conservation of earlier patterns of adaptation. We can think of language as being merely an expression of another neural contribution to the construction of mental imagery, analogous to the contributions of the encephalized sensory systems and

their association systems. *We need language more to tell stories than to direct action.* In the telling we create mental images in our listeners that might normally be produced only by the memory of events as recorded and integrated by the sensory and perceptual systems of the brain . . . . In hearing or reading another's words we literally share another's consciousness, and it is that familiar use of language that is unique to man.[19] (emphasis mine)

Language, then, is far more than a colorless medium of communication, more even than a system of signs, for it plays a continuous active role in the processes of imagining and interpreting the world. It is from this perspective on language that we can appreciate the richness of the Southeast Asian concept of sounding the texts. It is in the mind that the flow of sounds—music and language—can join with visual images, even shadows, in the process Rothenberg has called "world-making and self-making." The power to control the sounding of the text, as Twalen shows us, is the power to create the world.

5
Village Temple Systems

You do yet taste
Some subtleties o' the isle, that will not let you
Believe things certain.

William Shakespeare
The Tempest

The performances held in temples constantly highlight discrepancies between the ideal and real social worlds, in order to chastise the congregation and nudge them into a more perfect realization of the ideals celebrated by the sounding of the texts. The thousands of yearly temple activations are never mere ceremonies of complacent thanksgiving; there are always problems to be solved, as the many actors of the Middle World pursue their different interests. Through the power of the sounding of the texts, temples become instruments for reshaping the Middle World, as people are compelled to see themselves and the world in terms of their conformity to the profound realities of the texts. But at the same time, temples *are* the social order, the basic institutional structure, that regulates the flow of life on a daily basis. It is due to this dual nature of temples—organizing the affairs of daily life and at the same time reflecting that life in the mirror of the Indic texts—that they possess the power to alter the fundamental arrangements of social life. In this chapter we will consider the role of temples as bridges between the Worlds, as institutions which simultaneously create a particular social order and seek to transcend it.

It seems worthwhile to begin by suggesting that this dual nature of temples is related to the distinction between art and ritual and the different roles played by each in the context of temple performances. A common view of ritual holds that it is essentially a way of articulating—and

93

encouraging commitment to—a desired cultural order. As Sherrie Ortner put it recently, "a successful ritual should catch participants up in an active process," which can "engage them and draw them through the transformations of meaning/consciousness that the ritual embodies."[1] In general terms, rituals have to do with the perpetuation of particular orders from one generation to the next. As such, they are part of the normal flow of life. For example, the Balinese perform seven major rituals marking the stages of human life in a cycle beginning with birth and ending with the final assimilation of the soul into divinity. A successful ritual therefore is one which imposes an order and thereby puts an end to questions. Clifford Geertz noted this aspect of ritual in Balinese funeral rites, which "consist largely of a host of detailed little busy-work routines, and whatever concerns with first and last things death may stimulate is well submerged in a bustling ritualism".[2]

Art, on the other hand—and not only in Bali, but as a general principle—is not art unless it engages the reflexive consciousness. Herein lies the difference between art and ritual, a difference that is entirely subjective in the sense that it pertains to a mental attitude, but is also perfectly real, a difference in the nature of the awareness brought to an event. One can be surrounded by music, by the words of a storyteller, by works of visual art, and yet not be affected by them, not paying any attention, therefore not being artistically engaged. But the instant one does pay attention, one is involved in the experience of art.

Of course, the boundary between art and ritual is fluid and may easily be crossed. Victor Turner has shown the potential for liminal moments in any ritual, when "those being moved in accordance with a cultural script are liberated from normative demands, when they are, indeed, betwixt and between successive lodgements in jural political systems."[3] Liminality creates an opportunity for reflexivity; in Turner's words, the ability "to stand aside not only from one's own social position, but from all social positions." But it seems plausible to suggest that at such moments the ritual is transformed, in the mind of the participant, into drama—in other words, into art. Again, it is the quality of awareness that makes the difference.

The distinction between ritual and art is elaborated in an interesting way in the classification of performances for temple activations. This classification is based on the organization of space within the temple courtyards. The innermost sanctum is a walled rectangular courtyard, with shrines for visiting gods and spirits arrayed at the "uppermost" end (the direction facing the center of the island). In this sanctuary are held rituals and performances which are obligatory. Precisely which rituals are performed varies from temple to temple, according to its history and particular functions. All rituals or performances held in this part of the temple are called *wali* (offerings). At the opposite, seaward end of the

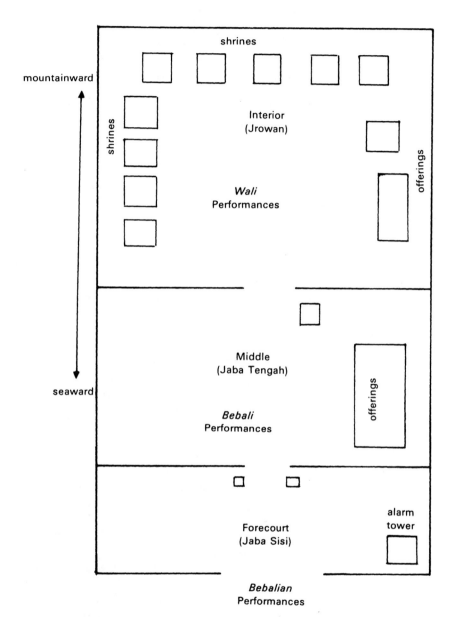

shrines

mountainward

shrines

Interior
(Jrowan)

offerings

Wali
Performances

seaward

Middle
(Jaba Tengah)

offerings

Bebali
Performances

alarm
tower

Forecourt
(Jaba Sisi)

Bebalian
Performances

Figure 5.1. Plan of a village temple—from the *Handbook for Temple Priests* (*Dasar Kepemangkuan*).

temple (considered closer to chthonic powers, hence more profane) are held offerings to the demons and performances termed *bebalian* (things to watch). They are put on entirely for the enjoyment of the human audience and are not obligatory—in a sense, they are separate from the true business of the temple activations. In between these two courtyards, the entrance and the inner sanctum, are one or more courtyards where *bebali* performances are held. This category includes most of the arts, from *gamelan* music to the sounding of the texts by poetry clubs, *wayang* puppeteers, actors, and dancers. *Bebali* performances, held in the middle courtyards, are intended to engage the interest of both the divine and human audiences (see Figure 5.1).

The boundary between *wali* and *bebali*, the inner and middle courtyards, is essentially the boundary between ritual and art. For example, a number of performances may be held in either the *wali* or *bebali* sections, but the nature of the performances are quite different. *Wayang* in the *bebali* area is performed as usual, with a screen and a constant stream of translations. But *wayang* held as *wali* in the inner courtyard proceeds without a screen and with no translations because the performance is addressed to the gods, for whom both would be superfluous. Most of the time no one other than the performers themselves pays any attention to *wali* performances.

But what is most intriguing about this Balinese classification is that it divides art and ritual into three categories rather than two. If *wali* is pure ritual, *bebalian* (in the outer courtyard) is pure performance. But most of the activity of a temple festival occurs in the middle region, where the boundaries of art and ritual are fluid, where gods from the inner courtyard and demons from the outer join the human audience, where "trance" is commonplace. In the middle region, not only gods and spirits, but demons, animals, and even the spirits of inanimate objects such as trees or pots may enter a person's body and take temporary control.

In *bebali* performances, there is an interesting ambiguity about the status of the actors. When the performance begins, they are actors, but they enact real "past" events and bring two cycles, two realms, within touching distance. Thus it is not surprising that the actors may often be "possessed" by the spirits of those they impersonate. Consider the Calonarang "witch dramas," well known from the descriptions by de Zoete and Spies,[4] Belo,[5] Mead,[6] and others. The story concerns an angry widow in an ancient Javanese kingdom who requests aid from the awful goddess Durga in order to combat a prince. She becomes an incarnation of Durga and engages in a prolonged battle with the king, and later on with a holy man. Eventually she is bested and sent to a celestial realm where she may be approached by modern witches who worship her as their queen. Her identity is thus multifaceted and is never fully realized at any single moment or event. Belo and Mead regarded her as perhaps the prime Balinese archetype, the "fear aspect of the Mother Figure"; but for the Balinese her various identities do not simply blend into a single archetype, they remain distinct. She is a real person who was once a widow, a candidate witch, an incarnation of Durga, and queen of all witches, who has reappeared to play a role in history many times since the eleventh century.

The story of the widow's incarnation as Durga forms the basis for the Calonarang drama, a *bebali* performance often held at festivals for the village "Death Temple" (or "innermost temple," Pura Dalem). The culminating moment of such performances is the appearance at midnight, from the inky depths of the temple, of a dancer costumed as the Calon Arang, the "candidate witch," who is treated as if she were real and may in fact become real, become a temporary incarnation of the witch herself.

There is an excitement in the Balinese theater, which is hard for us to appreciate, that derives from the fact that the boundaries between drama and magic, dance and ritual, and impersonation and reality are not fixed, and the principals of an ancient witch drama may take possession of their dramatic impersonators and renew their ancient battles on the stage. Or as with a Calonarang witch who suddenly became "possessed" and ran off toward the graveyard with the braver souls of the village in hot pursuit, the stage itself may dissolve (or, better, widen to include the audience). "Trance"—divine possession—is unpredictable; the audience does not know when the world before their eyes may melt away and their own bodies become vehicles for a god. Even in performances where trance is exceedingly rare, a member of the audience may become "entranced," although the actors do not. In inviting the gods to descend to their thrones in the temples, the villagers are inviting them to take an interest in their lives, and the world of the village may be spectacularly transformed into a stage on which nymphs, witches, and gods play out their own dramas. The boundaries between art and magic or ritual are always capable of shimmering away, hence the ambiguity of *bebali*.

It is perhaps easiest for us to comprehend this Balinese view of the world by watching the shadow world of the *wayang*, where villagers are constantly enlisted by the gods in their own quarrels, and every character and every stage or setting may be transformed by a flick of the *dalang's* (puppeteer's) wrist. Often in the midst of a scene, the image of a character will flicker insubstantially for a moment and then be replaced by a god, usually much to the discomfort of the other characters who had not seen through his incognito. Interludes in which the clowns, portrayed as peasants, talk about the story as *they* see it are a fixture of *wayang* performances, separate from their function as translators. Relations between the village and the worlds of Balinese cosmology are manifold and interpenetrating. And for the Balinese the arts do not merely describe these worlds within worlds, but invoke them, provide a means of access to them, and dissolve the boundaries between the illusory mundane world of the village and the multiple realities of which it is but a part.

VILLAGE TEMPLE SYSTEMS

In the oldest known inscriptions, the term used for "village" is *wanua*, a Malayo-Polynesian word that may date from the era of the first farming communities. In later inscriptions, the term *wanua* is gradually replaced by *desa*, a Sanskrit word for a civilized community. A Balinese *desa* is defined by a cluster of three temples (the "Three Great Temples", Kahyangan-Tiga). These temples define a particular sector of the Middle World in terms of its linkages to the Upper and Lower Worlds. Each of the three temples is associated with one of the three great divine principles of Hindu cosmology. The creative powers of the god Brahma are linked to the Origins Temple (Pura Puseh), in which the *desa* charter is kept if one exists. Such charters, sometimes supplemented by ancient royal inscriptions such as those described in Chapter 2, define the boundaries of the *desa* and set forth rules of customary law (*adat*) pertaining to the *desa*. Such rules vary considerably from one *desa* to another; what is appropriate in one *desa* may be strictly forbidden in its neighboring *desa*.

Adjacent to, or in some instances included within, the Origins Temple is the Great Council Temple (Pura Balai Agung), associated with the god Wiṣnu and hence with the forces of preservation and maintenance. In some villages the activations of this temple are coupled with meetings of the village heads, to regulate the rituals or political actions needed to ensure the continued prosperity of the village.

The last member of the triumvirate is the Inner Temple (*Pura Dalem*), associated with the chthonic aspects of the god Siwa and hence with the underworld and the forces of dissolution. This temple is usually located near a graveyard, at the seaward end of the village. Ideally, the locations of the three temples define the sacred space of the *desa*, with the Origins Temple and Great Council Temple at the uppermost (most sacred) end of the village, and the Inner Temple establishing a connection to the underworld at the lower end. The actual locations of these temples are seldom in perfect conformity to this scheme, but what is crucial is their collective ability to situate the territory of the *desa* in the context of the Three Worlds. The Three Great Temples are the foundation of any human settlement; they create the links to the other worlds which ensure the continuity of life in the Middle World.

Within the boundaries of a village as it is thus defined, three other major temple networks regulate most aspects of social life. They are the "neighborhood" or "ward" temples (*Pura Banjar*), the water temples, which were described in Chapter 2, and "caste" or "kinship" temples. A typical village will contain several dozen temples belonging to each of these networks and may in addition possess other temples such as those of royal or princely courts or temples associated with some special feature of the village or its territory. But to describe a village as consisting of independent networks of specialized temples is somewhat misleading, since the functions of temples often interlock. Perhaps the most significant aspect of this phenomenon has to do with the scheduling of temple activations. We saw in Chapter 2 that all water temples hold their festivals according to the *wuku* calendar, so that the ritual calendars of temples mesh with the 105-day growing season of Balinese rice. By holding festivals according to a permutational calender marking intervals of 35, 105, 210, and 420 days, the rituals of different temples could be scheduled to form a pattern maximizing the use of water across regions. It is therefore interesting that most other temples also hold their festivals according to the same calender of intervals—in other words, most temples hold festivals at intervals of 35, 105, 210, and 420 days. It also appears to be significant that those temples whose rituals are pegged to the older lunar calender (with festivals typically once a year, on a full moon) are by and large the older temples—an association noted by the Dutch archaeologist Goris many years ago.

But before we go any further, it is necessary to briefly review the functions of the major temple networks not so far described: the neighborhood temples (Pura Banjar) and "caste temples."

Banjars

A *banjar* consists of a temple, called the Pura Banjar or "Neighborhood Temple," and a meeting place adjacent to the temple that together bind a cluster of houseyards together into a formal "neighborhood" or *banjar*. Most of the houseyards in each *banjar* are located fairly close together, but often a few are situated some distance from the center of the *banjar*. *Banjar* are corporate groups: once each month, on a particular date fixed by the Sasikh calendar, the heads of each member household meet at the "*banjar* meeting pavillion" (*balai banjar*) to discuss all of the collective affairs of the *banjar*. Decisions are ordinarily reached by consensus. The matters that come before the *banjar* for decisions vary considerably. Since rice farming is controlled by the water temple system, *banjar* seldom have to make decisions about agriculture, while major political or kinship affairs are usually matters which go beyond the neighborhood level.

Banjars, then, are left to make whatever decisions affect the neighborhood that have not been preempted by some other organizations.

Matters that frequently came up in the many *banjar* meetings I attended in 1971 and 1974–1976 included keeping track of the participation of members in work groups formed to repair and maintain *banjar* property such as streets and buildings; admission of new members and discussion and implementation of orders from the government (schooling, family planning, statistical records, work groups, holding elections, etc.); formation and supervision of clubs, such as dance troupes and *gamelan* orchestras, and preparations for rituals and festivals, including the rites of passage of *banjar* members and the annual *banjar* temple festivals. *Banjars* choose chairmen, usually called *klian* (elders), who preside over the meetings and see that the decisions of the *banjar* are carried out. They are the link between the *banjar* members and higher political authority. They keep track of attendance at *banjar* meetings and work projects and may impose fines or sanctions on lateness or absence.

To belong to a *banjar*, a man must have a female relative who joins as his partner. Ideally a husband and wife constitute a unit, but sometimes boys may belong with their mothers or sisters, or girls with their fathers or brothers, because of a death or divorce. Sometimes single men may belong as "half members" (*tapukan*). Structures and procedures within any one *banjar* vary from village to village. For example, there may be more than one *klian*, and he may have assistants, elected or appointed by the *banjar*. Other *banjar* officers may include the heads of the *gamelan* orchestra and other associations (*sekehe*).

Banjar also have many important ritual duties. The festivals (*odalan*) of the *banjar* temple are important events in which every member household must participate. Dealing with the natural and supernatural forces that affect the life of the *banjar* is a collective responsibility—a fact made especially clear by the relationship of the *banjars* to death rituals. When someone dies, the *banjar* alarm hanging in the temple is sounded, and every household must send a member to the house of the dead to help with washing the corpse. It is then given a preliminary burial, except in special cases involving high-caste persons who are cremated immediately. Months or years later, when the corpse is disinterred and the remains are prepared for cremation, the *banjar* is again called on for help. *Banjars* are also often involved in other rituals of their members, such as marriages. But most of my informants considered the participation of the *banjar* in death rituals as its indispensable function, along with holding festivals in the *banjar* temple to ensure the prosperity of the neighborhood.

The origins of the *banjar* system are somewhat mysterious. Several Dutch ethnographers believe that the *banjars* began as "cults of the dead" in areas where the Hindu custom of cremation took hold among the people.

The word *banjar* is indigenous to Bali in origin and means "row" or "series." In the earliest inscriptions, *banjar* does not refer to a "neighborhood," but rather to a court official.

Kinship Temples

One of the most significant ideas borrowed from the Indic world was the concept of "caste" and the associated ideas of fate, *karma*, and social ranking. The Indic myths celebrated in the arts depicted human society as consisting of four major endogamous groups:

Brahmana, the highest caste, who could become priests
Ksatriya, the warrior-kings
Waisya, the lesser nobility and merchants
Sudra, the commoners, people without caste

This is the Varna system, in which each person's social rank or caste depends upon their actions in previous lives. According to the laws of *karma*, meritorious actions lead to rebirth at a higher rank. Ksatriya, then, are born to rule, while Brahmans are born to follow a spiritual life and Sudras to lead the lives of peasants.

The myths did not pay a great deal of attention to the intricate social and economic ties which sustain the Varna system in much of India, such as the *jati* hereditary exchange relationships within individual communities. Consequently, in Bali the foundation of the caste system came to be not an ongoing *jati* system of exchanges binding the caste groups in each community together, but rather the ideal model of the Varna system celebrated, in one way or another, by most of the Indic myths performed in temple festivals. This is an important point, for it is often suggested that the Balinese do not really have a caste system, which is to say that what the Balinese call caste is rather far removed from Indian caste systems. But neither the gods of conquest nor of economics ever laid down a template of caste for the Balinese. The Varna system came to Bali in conjunction with Hindu philosophy and the theory of divine kingship, as is evident from the early royal inscriptions. But despite these somewhat ephemeral origins, caste had very tangible consequences for Balinese society.

To begin with, the Varna image of a hierarchy of endogamous castes had to be reconciled with a kinship system that emphasized neither descent nor hierarchy. The Balinese kinship system is technically "Hawaiian," or "Generational," a system that would appear to preclude the formation of large endogamous descent groups (see Figure 5.2). In this system, the structurally simplest of all terminological systems, the word "father" includes all male relatives of the father's generation. "Mother," likewise, embraces all women of the mother's generation. The system

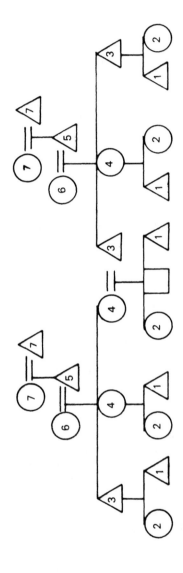

1: *bli* if older; *adi* if younger
2: *mbok* if older, *adi* if younger
3: *bapo* or *aji*
4: *meme*; if older than mother = *weh*
5: *kakiang* or *pekak*
6: *niang* or *dadong*
7: *kumpi*

Figure 5.2. Kinship terminology. This terminological system, technically known as "Hawaiian" or "Generational," makes use of only two distinctions: sex and generational status with respect to ego.

provides no clear way to distinguish lineal descent groups on either the father's or the mother's side. Moreover, the Balinese practice several customs that further obscure lineal relationships: the names of elders are tabooed, and personal names, teknonyms, are used in preference to them, so that two Balinese would find it difficult to trace a common ancestor even if they wanted to. Since it is impossible to trace one's ancestors more than a few generations back, it is also impossible to trace relationships horizontally beyond second cousins. The introduction of the Varna concept did not alter this system, which remained essentially intact; rather, caste became another institutional system, structured around temple networks.

In theory, the system works this way: upon marriage a woman joins the descent group of her husband and worships his ancestors at a small shrine in his house compound. Several households are typically linked by close kin ties (e.g., "brothers"), and in the "origin" or "oldest" house there is a higher-ranking shrine or temple (*sanggah gde*). In general all of the people who gather at this temple for periodic rituals are aware of their kinship relations with all the other members. But there are usually one or more temples (called *dadia, panti, paibon,* or *ibu*) of higher rank than the *sanggah gde* uniting several *sanggah gde* congregations, perhaps across several villages, whose members are aware of their status as members of the same descent group simply because they all worship at the same temple on the same day. Fathers bring their sons, sons their wives and children, and the knowledge of one's membership in such larger kinship units is passed on in the form of obligations to worship at, and support, particular temples.

The last and highest level of kinship temple is the *soroh* temple, considered to be the origin temple for a subcaste. (Like the Indians, the Balinese decompose the castes of the Varna system into numerous subcastes; the Brahmans, for example, are divided into seven subcastes, which are supposed to be ranked from "highest" to "lowest," although these rankings are not unanimously agreed on).

Temples, then, provided a means for coping with the generational kinship terminology and shallow genealogical reckoning of the indigenous Balinese kinship system by marking out a system of patrifiliative descent groups. Whether or not people can trace their precise relationships to other members of their caste groups, if they belong to the caste temple, then they belong (by definition) to the segment of the "caste" or "descent group" symbolized by the temple. In a sense, patrilineal descent lines are built "backwards" by the construction of temple chains, each temple symbolizing a descent group. And caste itself became not the basis for a new kinship system but one of the institutions of Balinese civilization organized by temple networks.

TEMPLES AND SOCIAL REALITY

Together with the water temples described in Chapter 3, the three varieties of temple networks described above—neighborhood temples, The Three Great Temples, and the Caste System temples—formed the institutions governing social life in rural Bali. With this background it is possible to discuss in a meaningful way the relationship of temples to social life in Balinese "villages."

In a sense, it *is* accurate to refer to *desa* (the unit defined by the Three Great Temples) as "villages." The Three Great Temples are the foundation of any social order; they connect a particular, bounded *place* with the forces from the other worlds in such a way as to make human life possible. But the Three Great Temples are only one of many groups of temples found in any village; they are in a religious sense the foundation of the community (as is implied in the title of one of the temples, the Pura Puseh or "Origins Temple"), but they are only one of the institutions of village life. Moreover, as James Boon observed, the members of the congregations of the Three Great Temples units are not always the residents of the region controlled by the temples.

> Ideally, a *desa* membership is the congregation of this triumvirate of temples. But there are sociological complications in this religious architecture of local organization. The congregation that supports a three-temple-cluster can contain people other than the residents of the geographical area under its influence. Thus, it is misleading to view the *desa* as a confederation of hamlets (*banjar*). One *desa* territory might contain residential units which are affiliated to another territory's three-temple-cluster. Or allegiances might even be divided between three-temple-clusters.... Thus, to see the *kahyangan tiga* even as a negatively defined "legal community" (C. Geertz 1959:1011), with distinctive purity/pollution rules and ritual detailing, although true in a broad sense, overlooks such cross-*desa* affiliations according to which persons attend three-temple-cluster ceremonies not as *banjar* members but as individual family heads with religious ties to that locality.[7]

It seems to be a basic principle of social order in Bali that ties to temples are always personal or individual: someone may live in one village and yet belong to, for example, one or two of the Three Great Temples in a different village.

Perhaps it may be useful to consider the village I lived in for a year and a half as a typically atypical Balinese community. Sukawati is first of all a *desa*, with a village charter and royal inscriptions that date back to the thirteenth century. Within the boundaries of this *desa* there are 52 major temples, of which most belong to the 4 varieties described above (see Figure 5.3). These 52 temples not only serve to carry on the day-to-day

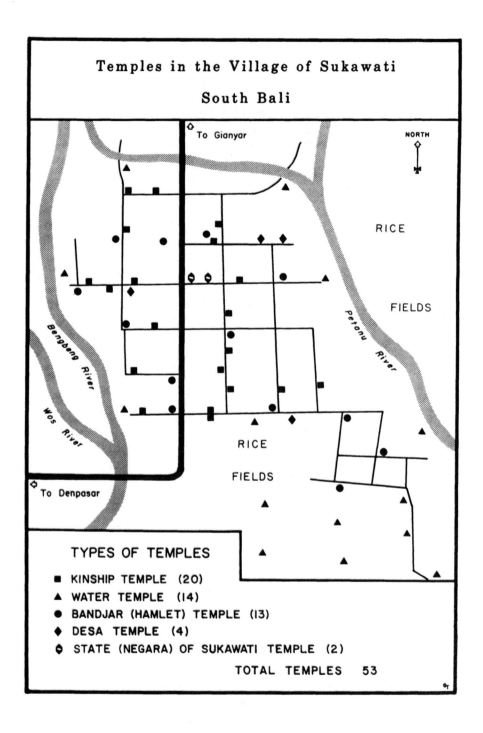

Figure 5.3. Temples in the village of Sukawati, South Bali

business of village life, with water temples organizing agricultural production, *banjar* temples carrying on the life of the 12 "neighborhoods" contained in the *desa*, and so forth, but they also link Sukawati to many institutions (and temples) elsewhere: to caste system temples all over the island; to water temples lying upstream all the way to the mountains; and others.

Several of the Sukawati temples do not belong to the four types described above: they are the temples of the royal dynasty that once ruled Sukawati as a *negara*, or "state." Thousands of people still come to these temples of a defunct political order every year. These are people who are "tied" to the Sukawati court temples because their ancestors were part of the *negara* of Sukawati, and they believe themselves to be reincarnations of their own ancestors. Thus, in a peculiar and uniquely Balinese way, the vanished kingdom of Sukawati periodically reappears as its temples are activated and the lords and subjects of Sukawati return to the Middle World, either as reincarnated humans or as spirits who are welcomed into their shrines in the temples. I have seen buses carrying hundreds of people arrive from dozens of different places on the island to help carry out these activations of the Sukawati royal temples 80 years after the state of Sukawati came to its end.

The apparition of a ghostly kingdom periodically appearing and then vanishing is something not all Balinese villages can boast of, but the caste system temples (which are found almost everywhere) evoke much the same questions as the appearances of the vanished court of Sukawati.

DEVIATIONS FROM THE IDEAL ORDER OF CASTE SYSTEM TEMPLES

The model of the caste system of Bali outlined above is clear, coherent, and generally agreed upon by articulate informants. Each major line of descent is memorialized in a series of temples, whose congregations form progressively more inclusive sets of patrilineally related kinsmen. Each unit in a caste system chain, from household shrines to all-island *soroh* (subcaste) temples, is activated at regular intervals when the kinsmen arrive to pay homage to the group's ancestors and gods in a temple festival. Kinsmen are also called upon to assist in major rites of passage such as marriages and funerals. One becomes a member of a caste by being reborn into it. Finally, the kinds of rituals (at birth, marriage, death, etc.) that each group can employ are strictly determined by their caste rank. In general, the higher the caste, the more exalted the ritual.

In reality, none of these generalizations is accurate. Many, perhaps most, Balinese do not belong to such ordered hierarchies of temples. Some do not belong to any caste system temples at all; others belong to one temple but have "lost track of" or "forgotten" the other temples to which they should be linked through this temple. Rather astonishingly, some people seem to try to compensate for their neighbors by belonging to two or even three subcastes at once! It is quite common for people to "change caste," perhaps several times in their lifetime. Again, the rituals employed by each caste group are anything but uniform. Finally, as I learned to my bewilderment one afternoon, a single caste system temple is sometimes used, on different days, by different subcaste units, which involves the complete reinterpretation of the symbolism of the temple's shrines. The contrast between the image of caste as a timeless order and the disorderly reality could not be more vivid.

Nor is this confusion only in the mind of the anthropologist, as may be made clear by an example. The Paseks are a cluster of subcastes of high-ranking "commoners." [James Boon has written extensively about the recent involvement of Pasek groups in modern Indonesian politics (Boon 1977).] Among their other activities, recently they have begun to issue a magazine or journal that is attempting to list all of the more important Pasek temples on the island. Each new issue lists more temples, together with the size of the temple congregation, its location, and the names of officials such as the temple priests. The preface to each issue of the journal provides the following diagram of the relationship of the size of each major type of temple to its name:

Pasek Temple Organization

Congregation Size	Type of Temple
	Catur Parhyangan (origin temple of Pasek subcaste)
1500 to 8000 families	Pura Agung
500 to 1500 families	Dadya Agung
100 to 500 families	Dadya
30 to 100 families	Panti
10 to 30 families	Paibon
1 to 10 families	Sanggah Kemulan

Reading through the descriptions of particular temples contained in the journal, I was impressed with the conformity between the size of the congregation and the name of title of the temple (Paibon, Panti, Dadya, etc.). However, on visiting a number of these temples, I discovered that the authors of the journal had taken the liberty of renaming each temple in conformity with this ideal diagram, usually without even notifying the temple congregation itself that the temple's name had been officially altered. In much the same way, the names of the temple priests were changed to conform to a new model, wherein the Pasek subcaste is entitled to an honorific title "I Gde" ("Great One"). Most of the priests were quite unaware that their names had been changed to reflect this new honor!

Such discrepancies between the ideal and the real are not a monopoly of the Paseks, who indeed may actually come closer to the ideal caste system temple network than any other group. Essentially, as we have seen, there are four possible ways in which individuals may not conform to the ideal relationship in a caste system temple chain: they may not belong to any temples at all, or belong to only one which is unconnected to the others of its subcaste, or belong to two or more different temple chains at once, or change their allegiance from one subcaste to another. Let us briefly consider each of these possibilities.

Not Belonging to any Caste System Temples

First, to belong to a caste system temple entails obligations of financial support: helping to carry out the temple festivals and participating in the rituals, such as marriages and deaths, of other members of the temple. Therefore, poor people often find it necessary to allow their ties to a caste system temple to lapse, sometimes permanently.

Second, low-ranking subcastes do not have any powerful incentive to participate in public rituals that serve only to proclaim their inferior status. Therefore, people who believe themselves to be of low subcaste (soroh) often permit themselves to "forget" their soroh. Consequently, temples for low-ranking soroh are relatively uncommon.

However, it is awkward to remain permanently in this state of nonaffiliation for two reasons. First, cremation rituals cannot be completed without symbolic insignia that proclaim the soroh rank of the deceased. Secondly, if someone simply decides to postpone cremation of one's forebears indefinitely, they become ghosts who are likely to become angry at this neglect and visit misfortunes on their descendants. The Balinese word kapongor means a calamity visited by angry, neglected ancestors who have not received their ritual due. Not to be cremated properly prevents them from reaching heaven and is thought to be a prime cause of kapongor.

Belonging to Only a Single Caste System Temple

It is also not uncommon for whole groups of people to lose track of their soroh, and thus of other branches of kinsmen. Ordinarily, such links are maintained by sending delegations to the big Origin Temple festivals of the *soroh*. But poor or remote temple groups may allow such ties to lapse simply by failing to send delegations. Alternatively, some groups would prefer to forget an embarrassingly low *soroh* status. But do these groups remain forever "lost"? No. Altering one's position in the *soroh* hierarchy is astonishingly easy. "Lost" individuals or groups need only visit various temples until they find one where they feel the presence of receptive ancestors. They then present themselves to the temple congregation and request permission to join on the basis of this revelation of their true ancestry.

Larger groups sometimes proceed in a more systematic search for their origins. Many Brahman residences (*griyas*) maintain libraries of *soroh* histories (*babads* or *prasasti*) that are consulted to try to match them against whatever the lost group remembers of its history. Perhaps the most famous of these libraries is kept in the ancient capital of Gelgel. I attended a sequence of rituals performed there, by which a lost group from an offshore islet was integrated into a middle-to-high Balinese *soroh*. At the end of these ceremonies, which occupied several days, the leader of the group was given a brief version of his *soroh* history, inscribed on copper plate, to be placed in the group's temple on the islet.

Belonging to Two or More Subcastes at Once

One group of members of the Pasek *soroh* in the village of Sukawati followed a nobleman into exile in the late nineteenth century and eventually settled some distance from Sukawati, in the region of Klungkung. In their new village they moved into a house formerly belonging to a family of the Pande (Smith) subcaste. Like all Balinese houses, this house contained a shrine for the ancestors of the Pande family, who continued to visit the shrine on their regular schedule even though the house was no longer occupied by their descendants. The Sukawati Pasek family, not wishing to risk angering spirits, seized this opportunity to become members of the local branch of the Pande group, performing the proper rituals to welcome the arriving Pande ancestors, who were in this way retroactively incorporated into their own family tree.

When their political position vis-à-vis their former homeland of Sukawati improved, they began to return to Sukawati for periodic visits and revived their family ties with the Paseks of Sukawati. The current head of this family group regards his Pasek temple in Sukawati as his "*kawitan pokok*," or principal origin place, to which he often returns for major festivals. But in his present home of Klungkung he celebrates all Pande temple festivals and is regarded as a "Pande Pasek," a sort of hybrid. His house has shrines for both sets of ancestors: the original Pande *sanggah gde* ancestral shrine and a Pasek "branch" (*nuntun*) shrine. Such arrangements are not uncommon, although one Sukawati resident who claimed allegiance to *three* subcastes was regarded by his neighbors as rather extravagant!

Logically, as the Balinese themselves will cheerfully concede, it is impossible for one family to belong to two or three *soroh* simultaneously. Obviously one cannot have two or three complete sets of ancestors on one's father's side. The *soroh* system of subcastes and the kinship system are therefore separable. *Soroh* allegiance is not really thought of in diachronic terms, in terms of one's actual descent, but rather in terms of the present: present status, present duties to ancestors and ghosts, and present temple obligations. So, belonging to two *soroh* simply translates into supporting more temple festivals and rituals and having more "kinsmen."

Changing One's Subcaste (*Soroh*)

Santo is a farmer who was born into a small "subcaste" named Moning, which boasts a total of only three temples on the entire island. When he married, houseland was scarce, so he moved into a house which had formerly belonged to a Pasek in his neighborhood, after having received permission from his *banjar* (neighborhood assembly). He erected a Moning shrine next to the two Pasek shrines already in existence in the houseyard. But things went badly for him; as his neighbors remember, he was forever weeping. So, on the advice of a curer-priest (*balian*), he renounced his Moning heritage and became a Pasek and soon became happy. There was at that time only one other Pasek family in his neighborhood (*banjar*), though the Monings were numerous. Santo became "brother" to this Pasek, whose family origin shrine (*sanggah gde*) was in Santo's houseyard.

Such adjustments are part of the normal social process in Bali and are not looked upon as religious crises. More spectacular versions of this process occur when someone tries to promote himself some distance up the subcaste hierarchy by actually renouncing his old subcaste in favor of another. In Sukawati, a very prosperous merchant who had allied himself to several powerful political friends discovered in a dream that a mistake had been made at the time of his birth. He was in reality not a true member of the low-ranking subcaste into which he had been born, but was in fact a reincarnated prince. He proposed to visit many princely temples until he found one in which he felt the presence of his true ancestors, and in the meantime suggested to the people of Sukawati that he be addressed as "Gusti" ("Prince"). This suggestion met with some disfavor, particularly among the remaining princes of Sukawati who could trace their descent link by link to the seventeenth century. Ultimately his claims were rejected, but only after many alarums and excursions.

CONCLUSION

We began this chapter by examining the institutional structures created by temple networks. In the village of Sukawati, 52 temples organize everything from neighborhood road repairs, to death rites, to the schedule of rice planting. But the ideal order celebrated in temple festivals is not always in perfect conformity to the on-the-ground reality. This was especially clear in the temples of the caste system, in which the ideal of an immutable social hierarchy contrasts rather vividly with the reality of people belonging to no castes or two at once and changing their caste more easily than their place of residence.

It is my contention that we cannot understand caste in Bali, or more generally the social order created by temples, without focusing on the interplay of art and ritual in temple festivals. To simply describe the operations of caste in Bali in customary anthropological fashion is to implicitly accept the claim of ritual, that the order of caste is timeless and immutable. But the "timeless" order of caste is itself the product of art—the sounding of the texts. Among the 10,000 islands of Indonesia, Bali is the only one which is home to a caste system. One might argue that the Balinese version of caste is not a true caste system, which is to say that it differs from the various versions of caste found in India. But caste in Bali is perfectly real, not only as an image of social order but as a complex system of temples, titles, rites, priveleges, and rules of behavior. The sounding of the texts created the Balinese caste system, in an almost literal sense lifting it off the pages of the Hindu epics and implanting it in the minds of the builders of temples.

The conclusion seems inescapable that the fluidity of caste, and of social life in general, is the outcome of the intertwining of art and ritual in temple festivals. The metaphor of intertwining—of separate strands interwoven—is significant, because art and ritual pursue different ends. Ritual, as ritual, insists that its order is timeless, while art—the sounding of the texts—requires that it be created with full awareness of the existence of alternatives. From this fruitful paradox emerges the Middle World, a world both real and imagined.

6
Bali Aga:
The Order of Time

My charms crack not, my spirits obey, and Time
Goes upright with his carriage.
William Shakespeare
The Tempest

One of the enduring mysteries of Balinese ethnography has been the existence of a group of villages which appear to diverge in several important ways from the patterns of social order common over the rest of the island. In the Balinese language, the inhabitants of these anomalous villages are called wong Bali Aga or wong Bali Mula ("Mountain Balinese" or "Original Balinese"). Everyone else is termed *wong Maospahit* ("Majapahit People").

This distinction was picked up by Dutch ethnographers in the colonial era and immediately became the center of a controversy which has continued to the present. According to the original Balinese explanation, recorded by ethnographers such as Korn and Goris, the wong Maospahit are the descendants of the legendary Majapahit Javanese "conquerors," while the *wong Bali Aga* are the descendants of the original Balinese who pride themselves on having successfully resisted conquest or assimilation by the Javanese. But this explanation carries the unlikely historical implication that the vast majority of the present Balinese population are actually transplanted Javanese, while the real Balinese survive in only a handful of remote villages.

There is, therefore, a temptation to reject the distinction entirely as an historical fable, but unfortunately, dismissing the distinction will not also dismiss the Bali Aga, who are, after all, chiefly celebrated for their determination not to disappear. Most of the major Dutch ethnographies of Bali, including Korn's classic *Adatrecht*, are organized around the distinction between these two types of villages.[1] Korn termed the majority type of village of the wong Maospahit "apanage," emphasizing their subordinate relationship to the indigenous aristocratic courts of precolonial Bali.

There have been essentially two explanations proposed for the existence of the Bali Aga, which in different ways take into account the fact that these villages tend to be located in relatively remote areas.[2] Korn suggested that it was the absence of courtly influence that led to the preservation, among the Bali Aga, of old-style customs and forms of social organization. Clifford Geertz has argued more recently that the Bali Aga are simply random variants produced by different environmental circumstances, arguing that mountain villages (which the Bali Aga mostly are) might well be expected to possess different customs than the lowland villages.

Neither of these explanations is quite satisfactory. Contrary to Korn's ideas, it may be argued (as Geertz has) that the island is simply too small to permit the sort of isolation that Korn suggests took place. In over a thousand years of Indic civilization in Bali, it stretches credibility to propose that the Bali Aga are fossil remnants of pre-Indic Balinese society. Contrary to Geertz, it may be observed that widely separated Bali Aga villages share a distinct cluster of characteristics that are not easily explainable by reference to the mountain environment in which most of them are found.

I propose that the differences between the Bali Aga and what I shall simply call "ordinary villages," of the sort described in the last chapter, are founded on the different role of temples in these two types of village. In ordinary villages, as we saw in the last chapter, temples perform two functions. Networks of temples link people from different villages in complex regional institutions, such as the water temple system, which organize aspects of social life. At the same time, temple festivals are instruments for reshaping the social world through the medium of artistic performances. Both of these functions are absent in Bali Aga temples. Temples do not link the members of their congregations to institutions that transcend the boundaries of the village. They are, instead, entirely inward looking. The village itself is a single, holistic institution, and village temples represent component parts of this institution. Secondly, temple festivals held in Bali Aga temples are exclusively of the type called *wali*: performances addressed to the gods and held in the innermost sanctum. There are no *bebali* or *bebalian* performances, no outside troupes of artists invited to perform, nor are Brahman high priests employed in the rituals. The very languages needed for such performances are unknown—the sole language used both in daily life and in ritual performances is Balinese. There are no reading clubs, no texts, and therefore, no sounding of the texts. Consequently, the phenomena of reflexivity and the merging of different realms in the liminal spaces of the temple does not develop.

Instead, temple performances reflect a very different vision of the world, based on the concept of the regularity of time cycles. Here, the theory of cyclical time, common to many Southeast Asian societies, becomes the basis, or image, of social order. The implications of this fact for anthropological theory are interesting. Like many societies, the Bali Aga find a model for their social order in what they perceive to be the order of nature. Following in the footsteps of Claude Lévi-Strauss, anthropologists have discovered many societies whose social classification scheme or taxonomy reflects their images of the natural order: nature and culture as reciprocal models. The Bali Aga, however, appear to find a model of social order not in the *things* of nature, but in what they perceive to be the natural order of time. They abstract from nature not its spatial relations or differences between species, but temporal structures. Social order is created, for the Bali Aga, by structures of cyclic progression—the same cycles that bring order to the Bali Aga universe. The festivals of Bali Aga temples invoke and display this vision of temporal harmony, which gives to life in these villages an extraordinary quality of timelessness. Temple activations persuasively articulate the idea that change always occurs in cycles, which are endlessly repeated or duplicated, so that ultimately both the social world and the cosmos are joined in a kind of moving equilibrium.

SOCIAL ORGANIZATION OF THE BALI AGA

In many Indonesian societies social status is determined in part by generational seniority. But in Bali Aga villages seniority is the dominant principle of social organization, paramount in every organization from dance clubs to the village leadership.

The most important institution is the *krama desa* (literally, "honored village elders"), to which all married couples belong. The inscriptions of the early Indic period (ninth to twelfth centuries) were usually addressed to the Ra Ama or *krama*, the "honored elders," and in Bali Aga villages the *krama* continue to rule.

This village organization is clearly symbolized in the meeting place for the *krama desa*, the Balai Agung, which is composed of an arrangement of several roofed platforms (*balai*) that are surrounded by a wall within a large open courtyard (see Figure 6.1). The Balai Agung (Great Balai) has buildings to house the *gamelan* orchestra and dancers, places for offerings to be prepared and displayed, and two long parallel *balai* for seating the

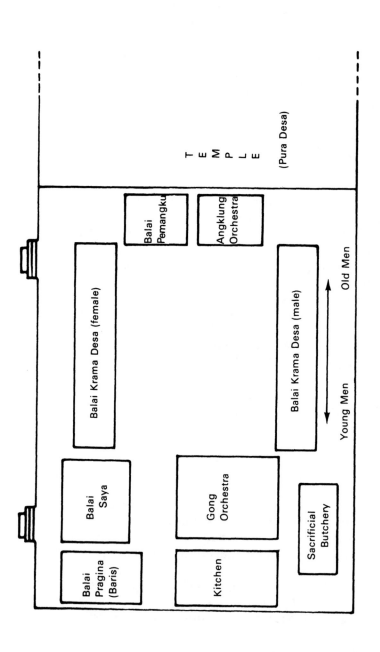
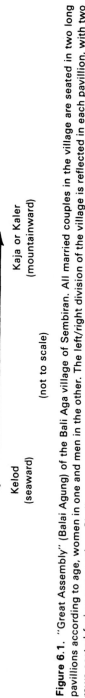

Figure 6.1. "Great Assembly" (Balai Agung) of the Bali Aga village of Sembiran. All married couples in the village are seated in two long pavillions according to age, women in one and men in the other. The left/right division of the village is reflected in each pavillion, with two rows seated facing one another. Similar arrangments prevail in other Bali Aga villages.

krama desa, one on the left for women, and one on the right for men. Both *balai* are aligned so that they point toward the sea at one end (*kelod*) and toward the mountain top at the other (*kaja* or *kaler*). The entire married population of the village is seated in two rows along these *balai* in a generational hierarchy, with the most recently married couple at the seaward end and the oldest married couple, ritual heads of the village, seated at the mountainward end. In some villages, the right and left rows in each *balai* are named. This right/left division in the seating arrangements symbolizes a dual division in each village structure, which is also mentioned in some of the early Indic inscriptions (viz. Srokadan B, 1321 A.D.). In such villages, men usually sit on the side their fathers sat, and wives follow their husbands, but in some villages an official (the Panyarikan) is empowered to change people's positions to ensure equal numbers on both sides.

As time goes by and new members join the *desa,* each couple's seats gradually move up. Every position in the seating has a title, accompanying special duties and responsibilities in village affairs. The oldest men are the leaders. In the village of Jullah (mentioned in three of the earliest extant inscriptions, ninth century), upon joining the *krama desa* a man is allotted farmland belonging to the village. After about ten years, the man may rise in the village hierarchy by having newly married men take seats behind him, and he is given a different patch of land; a new member gets his old land. This rotation continues, at ten year intervals, until he dies, retires, or is expelled from the village. Jullah seems to be the only village where such a system of communal land ownership still exists. But in the village of Sembiran, near Jullah, land was controlled by descent groups and was passed on by inheritance until about 15 years ago. Final authority over rights to land, however, rested with the *krama desa.*

Perhaps the most distinctive characteristic of Bali Aga villages, then, is the power of the *krama desa,* which in part derives from its control of productive land. But there are slight variations in village structure.

Jullah

Jullah is located near the north coast, on the fringes of the former court of Buleleng. Mentioned in several inscriptions as early as the ninth century, it is today a highly conservative, wealthy, and traditional example of a Bali Aga village. The village membership is divided into two groups, the east and west sides. The nominal village leaders are the two eldest married men, one from the east side and the other from the west. Seated at the mountainward end of the *krama desa* platform, these men, the *kabayans* of the east and west, are heads of the village as well as senior priests who

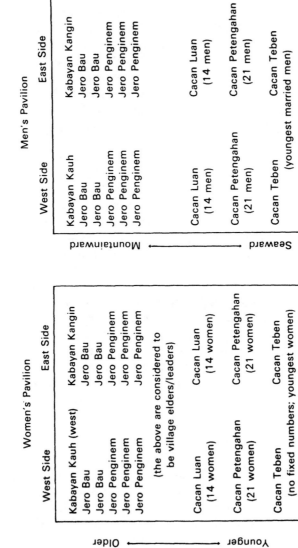

Figure 6.2. Village Membership (*krama desa*) of the Village of Jullah, according to seating arrangements in the Village Assembly Pavilions (Balai Krama Desa)

supervise the village temple festivals. Any man may become *kabayan* if he and his wife live long enough and are not expelled for infraction of village rules.

Ranking below the *kabayans* are a number of other named positions, which every villager may eventually hold. The duties and titles of these officials vary somewhat from village to village. The hierarchy for Jullah is displayed in Figure 6.2. The oldest men are responsible for leading the meetings of the *krama desa* and organizing and executing village temple festivals and other rituals. Middle-aged and younger men do the work and may play for the orchestra or dance at the festivals.

Jullah was visited by F. A. Liefrinck in 1889, when only North Bali had been brought under colonial rule. He reported that

> the land lying to the east of Cape Pondjok-Baroe, known as "East Pondjok," has a very different character than the greater part of Buleleng [North Bali], being a desolate and uninhabited area . . . . Here are the villages . . . where the bond among the inhabitants is still the strongest, where the strangers are as much as possible kept out, at least entirely kept out of the arrangements of the desa.
>
> One such there is Djoelah, a desa which has already existed for many centuries. The territory of the desa is not large, and the grounds, which are well situated, are cultivated year in and year out with djagung, cotton, legumes and tobacco. The terrain is gently sloping, but through lack of irrigation water no rice terraces [*sawah*] exist. All fields remain the property of the desa, and belong therefore, to all inhabitants. They are divided equally between members of the desa. Every ten years they are redivided, the last time in 1886 . . . . [3]

Sukhawana

Sukhawana is located in the central mountains, near the crater of Mount Batur. The dual division is invested with greater significance here: rather than "east" and "west," the halves are called *siba kiwa* (left) and *siba tengen* (right), and the *kabayan* from the right side is the *desa* leader. The right side is considered "higher." Where one sits is determined by birth. The elders of both sides, a group of 24 couples, are responsible for carrying out ceremonies at the numerous village-owned temples. Ordinary village members take turns helping with these ceremonies and send offerings but are not required to be present at every ceremony, as are the elders.

Beneath the upper division are the Pergina groups, consisting of a *gamelan* orchestra group, a *baris* dance group, and the lowest group, which is responsible for making food and other preparations for village temple festivals.

Sukhawana Desa Hierarchy

Elders	
Kabayan Kiwa (left)	Kabayan Tengen (right)
Jero Bau	Jero Bau
Jero Bau	Jero Bau
Jero Singukan, 1–4	Jero Singukan, 1–4
Jero Pengalanan, 1–3	Jero Pengalanan, 1–3
Jero Penyarikan, 1–2	Jero Penyarikan, 1–2
Ordinary Members	
Pergina Gong (*gamelan* group)	
Pergina Baris (dance group)	
Sekehe Hebat (preparations for ceremony group)	

Thus, upon marriage a couple joins the *sekehe hebat* and gradually progresses through the dance and music groups to the upper, most prestigious positions. At different times in their lives, each person becomes a worker, dancer, musician, and priest. However, if either husband or wife dies, the remaining partner is given a special title (*selain*) and is retired from the *desa* membership. Also if all one's children are married, one receives the title *bakhi* and is excused from all village work. Husbands and wives always have the same rank in the village hierarchy.

Sembiran

Sembiran is located about three kilometers to the southwest of Jullah. It is also a very old village, on the site of megalithic remains including a pyramid with stone at its crest (recently destroyed) and stone tools. It is mentioned in ninth century inscriptions. The *desa* hierarchy is

Elders	Ordinary Members
Jero Siut	Jero Bahan
Jero Kabayan	Jero Jahiya
Jero Bau	Jero Panakawan
Jero Sendukan	Jero Pamuhit

In Sembiran there is less emphasis on the right-left division, but the seating arrangements are identical to those in the other two villages: a long *balai* with men seated on either side, and a similar *balai* for the women. Figure 6.1 reproduces the ground plan of the Balai Agung in Sembiran. On the long platform on the right are seated the male members of the *krama desa*, *kabayans* at the "higher" (*kaja*) end. The wives are seated on the left *balai* in the same order as their husbands. In front, there are two *balais*: one for the *angklung gamelan*, the other for the priests. When the village meeting begins, the older men move to this *balai*, symbolizing their status as priests. Immediately behind them, as they face the village, is the Pura Balai Agung, the village temple.

There are many similarities between the organization of Bali Aga villages and the organization of early villages as inferred from the royal inscriptions. In the earliest inscriptions, royal commands are addressed to the *tuha-tuha rama*, or "honored elders," and the *kabayans* are often specifically mentioned. In later inscriptions, from the thirteenth and fourteenth centuries, a more complete list of village officials or leaders is often included. All such lists correspond closely to contemporary Bali Aga village hierarchies. Srokadan B (1343 A.D.), for example, is addressed to the *tuha-tuha rama* (honored elders), composed of the *kabayans* and *bahus* of the left and right: precisely the same hierarchy as Sukhawana today. As if to underscore the point, these "honored elders" are further identified by teknonyms (e.g., "Kabayan of the Right, Grandfather of Warnasa"), which reiterate—as it were, metonymically!—the generational principle. Thus it would seem, on this evidence, that the fundamental "gerontocratic" structure of Bali Aga villages is pre-Indic.

KINSHIP ORGANIZATION AND TIME CYCLES

The structure of kinship organizations (descent groups) in Bali Aga villages provides a particularly clear example of the preeminence of the principle of temporal order. As we saw in the preceding chapter, Balinese kinship terminology is technically Hawaiian or Generational, and the generational emphasis is enhanced by the use of teknonyms and the phenomenon Clifford Geertz terms "genealogical amnesia," whereby the names of elders are tabooed and deliberately forgotten. However, despite their reluctance to actually trace their descent beyond two or three generations, Bali Aga villagers nonetheless divide themselves into "descent groups" based, in theory, on a group called *nyama tunggal kawitan* ("kinsmen of a single origin"). Figure 6.3 shows the theoretical structure of such group, which consists of first male patricousins and their patrilineal "core line" of descent. Elsewhere in Bali, these "kinsmen of an origin" can

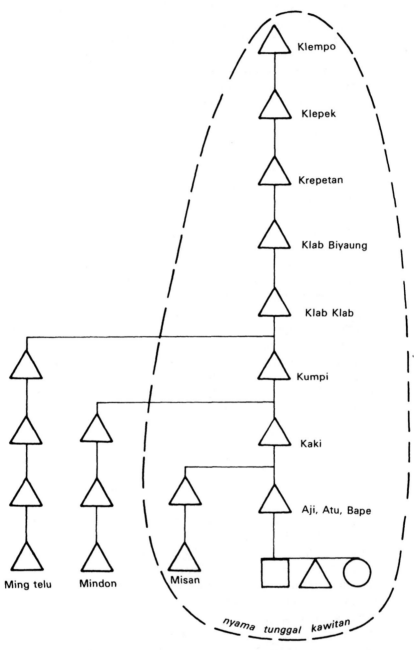

Figure 6.3. Members of *nyama tunggal kawitan* ("kinsmen of a single origin"), Village of Sembiran.

become a corporate descent group (in Geertz's terminology, a *dadia*) by constructing a public temple for ancestor worship. These are the groups that assume caste titles and compete for the privileges of rank with other *dadia* (descent groups) in the villages of the sort described in the last chapter. However, as we saw, membership in such descent groups is quite flexible, even optional, so that many persons remain outside this framework of caste and descent groups for periods of time.

But in the Bali Aga villages, *dadia* are neither optional nor competitive, nor are they truly kinship units. In Sembiran and Jullah, it is customary for a man to belong not only to his father's *dadia*, but also to his mother's and possibly to his wife's as well. He may join yet another *dadia*, in addition to these three, in order to enlist the support of its ancestor spirits. Thus, while Sembiran boasts 23 *dadia*, in principle anyone may belong to any of them. Members of a *dadia* who are not kinsmen of a single origin (i.e., not patrilineally related to *dadia* ancestors) are termed "additional" (*sampingan*) members, but are considered to be full members of the *dadia*, taking part in all *dadia* rituals and meetings. Indeed, the head of each dadia, its *kabayan* (*oldest* married man), may belong to the additional group! One young man belongs, for example, to three *dadias*: his father's, mother's, and wife's. In his father's *dadia*, he and the other 6 patrilineally related kinsmen of the same origin are outnumbered by approximately 90 additional members, one of whom is the *dadia* head! (However, each *dadia* must have a Panyarikan (Secretary) and Pemangku (Priest) who are true kinsmen of a single origin.) The distinction between the two types of *dadia* members is not unknown to the villagers; rather, it is systematically deemphasized. This is clearly seen on the day when *all* Sembiran *dadias* hold their temple festivals. Beginning early in the morning, *dadias* hold their festivals in rotation until late in the evening, when the last festival is to be concluded. In this way, each person can participate in the rituals of several *dadias*, one after another. The ongoing theme of the subordination of the *dadias* to the *krama desa* (village gerontocracy) is carried forth in a special temple (Pura Desa Gde) in which heads of dadias meet once a year for a village temple festival.

The *dadia*, then, is a curious hybrid, in which the logic of descent gives way to the logic of temporal order. The potential hierarchy within *dadias* and between *dadias* is not permitted to develop (as it does elsewhere in Bali). In its place remains the hierarchy of generation, the only hierarchy allowed to exist.

RITUAL AND THE ARTS

The rites of passage are very simple in Bali Aga villages. Marriage is accomplished by elopement or abduction, then confirmed when kinsmen of the groom pay a brideprice to the girl's father and the marriage is reported to the Panyarikan. After this, the couple receive their new names and take their places at the monthly meetings of the *krama desa*. Death rituals are even simpler. The corpse is washed by kinsmen, offerings are made, and then the corpse is placed in a pit or simply left on the ground in a "cemetery" a short distance from the village. (This custom has recently been discouraged by the Indonesian government and is now practiced in only a few villages. In one village, it has become a tourist attraction, and so will probably continue!)

The Bali Aga seem to be saving their energies for the temple festivals, which are celebrated with gorgeous offerings, feasting, music, and dance.

Temple activations are set, in the Bali Aga villages, by the Hindu-Balinese lunar calendar rather than by the Hindu-Javanese *wuku* calendar. To celebrate these events, Bali Aga villages customarily possess a large, often ancient, *gamelan* orchestra. The *gamelan*, which belongs to the whole village, is considered sacred, and there are important restrictions on its use. Under ordinary circumstances it may not leave the village and may only be played for village temple festivals. The ethnomusicologist Jap Kunst, in his survey of *gamelans* in Java and Bali, discovered that the ancient *gamelan selonding* ensembles are now almost exclusively confined to the villages of the Bali Aga.[4] As Kunst observes, the antiquity of the *selonding* is confirmed by five royal inscriptions, dating from around the twelfth century, instructing villages owning *selondings* to pay a special tax.

The operators of this *gamelan* are not necessarily musical enthusiasts; they are rather those members of the *krama desa* whose generational rank within the village places them, for a time, in the *gamelan* section of the village hierarchy.

Most dances are performed either by those whom time and age has placed in the "dance" section of the *krama desa* or by the young unmarried boys and girls of the village, who are organized into two sections for this purpose. The dances may be quite simple. At a temple festival in the village of Jullah, the young men of the village divide into two groups, according to whether they belong to the Left or Right side of the village, and face each other in pairs for a moment in front of a shrine in the main village temple while wearing warrior costumes and holding lances. The "dance" is called *ngigel pamit*, the "dance of asking leave". It is one of a large number of dances called *baris* (martial dances) that are performed by men. A survey of mountain villages by Beryl de Zoete and Walter Spies in the 1930s found over 20 different kinds of ceremonial *baris*, "some peculiar to one village, some to another, and forming an essential part of every temple feast."[5]

In 1933, Claire Holt observed an odd variety of *baris*, called Baris Jangkang, performed in only a few tiny settlements on the island of Nusa

Penida.⁶ Three times each 35-day month, on the fourth, eighteenth, and twenty-fourth day, the Jangkang was performed inside the temple of a particular *dadia* (descent group). Dressed as warriors, 9 men danced briefly with lances and swords to the accompaniment of music from 2 drums and 4 small cymbals. In 1976 I found this dance being performed precisely on schedule.

The women's dances of the Bali Aga closely resemble the men's, recast in feminine, unmartial mold. Lines of beautifully dressed dancers, arranged in generational files, dance slow steps before the shrines inside the temple courtyard. Some are performed by the unmarried girls, others by all the women belonging to the temple congregation. *Mendet* and *gabor* offer flowers or other gifts to the gods, while other dances, such as *redjang*, offer only the dancer herself.

Some dances, such as the Mabuang ("Libation dance"), involve everyone. During their survey of Bali Aga dances in the 1930s, de Zoete and Spies observed this dance in a mountain village:

> The Maboeng (libation ceremony) at Asak was preceded by a slow impressive dance (Nameang), in which all of the young men of the village took part, brilliant as a bunch of parrots, with gorgeous cloth-of-gold headcloths and golden flowers in their hair ... they advanced with great solemnity in close rows, the right hand on the hip, the left stretched alternately forward to the side. Each leg in turn was slowly raised, brought forward and held in front, very much turned out, then placed on the ground, while the other was immediately lifted and placed beside it but slightly apart .... For the Maboeng they formed in two long rows, sitting on the ground, and grouped according to the colour of the headcloths. Between the rows one man sat pouring out toeak (rice wine) in front of another who chanted as he swayed to and fro .... These ceremonies have a more or less recurrent character, and are repeated with slight variations all day and all night, during the duration of the feast.⁷

CONCLUSION

Dances such as the Jangkang, performed in identical fashion three times a month in a tiny, isolated hamlet, assert a particular relationship between living men and their ancestors and gods. Like the great slow dances of the generations in other Bali Aga villages, such dances may be addressed to the ancestor-gods, but on a deeper level they are hymns to the great god Chronos. Bali Aga culture is built on a view of time as the great bringer of order, the order of slow and predictable changes. This view is proclaimed in the language of ritual and dance and exemplified in all phases of social life.

Among the Bali Aga, it is believed that villagers are always reborn into the same village, unless they commit some great crime for which they are exiled forever. The village is therefore, in a sense, eternal: just as the land and temples are always there, so the villagers, after a short spell in heaven as "ancestors," return to the village to be reborn. People are in this sense exactly like rice or other plants, they say that "after harvesting, the seeds are replanted."

The village is self governed by a strict gerontocracy. Upon marriage, a young couple sits at the seaward end of a long ceremonial pavilion. They are given a plot of farmland and a house in the village. After about ten years, as other young couples join the village after them and take their seats behind them, the land is redistributed. As one gets older, one's land improves and one's seat moves up the hierarchy of authority. Each seat or group of seats has a particular title and function attached to it, from "butchers" at the seaward end to "village head" at the mountainward end. The formal heads of the village, who also function as temple priests, are the two oldest married couples. All major decisions are made by the entire community, led by the elders.

In such a system, one's age in absolute terms is almost a meaningless concept, since each person has lived through the entire cycle of statuses from "newborn" to "elder village head" to "ancestor spirit" and back to "child" many times. On the other hand, one's *relative* age (relative to other villagers) determines one's social position.

Indeed, the social order of Bali Aga villages is, in a fundamental sense, created by the order time brings. Individuals derive their social position, their status, and their responsibilities vis-à-vis other villagers and also the village as a corporate unit from their place in the generational hierarchy. Even one's name fixes one's place in this progressive hierarchy, and names are inexorably altered as time brings changes in one's relative position. Not only the village (krama desa), but *all* social organizations in Bali Aga villages derive their structure from the order time creates. Hence the otherwise inexplicable structure of kinship groups (dadia), wherein the position of the leader (kabayan) falls to the oldest man, even if he is not a member of the lineal descent group.

The performances held within Bali Aga temples proclaim that this social order mirrors the natural order, by drawing everyone and everything into the endlessly repetitive time-cycles which are, for them, the order of the cosmos. Here there are no liminal spaces, no images of other rules or other kinds of order, and hence no cultivation of reflexive awareness. The social world is in a state of being, not becoming, and the arts mirror its ancient pattern of order. In so doing, they both construct and perpetuate this worldview, with all its consequences for social life.

It is interesting to speculate on the likely effects of encouraging *bebali* artists to perform in Bali Aga temple festivals. If my arguments are correct, the sounding of the texts in such performances would eventually transform these villages into conventional Balinese villages. Temples would be redefined as branches of Middle World institutions. Performers would attempt to confront villagers with the question of their places in the cosmological framework of the Middle World. The whole procession of gods, heroes, Brahmans, and demons would be conjured out of the texts, and the contours of the world would change.

7
Eka Dasa Rudra: Cycles of the Middle World

The cloud-capped towers, the gorgeous palaces, the solemn temples, the
  great globe itself,
Yea, all which it inherit, shall dissolve.

William Shakespeare
The Tempest

The ceremony *taur* Eka Dasa Rudra ("offering to the Eleven Rudras"),
which is supposed to be held at the close of every century on the Icaka
calendar, provides a particularly interesting illustration of the role of
temple performances in shaping the social world of Bali. To begin with, it is
the greatest of all Balinese temple festivals and is concerned not with any
single institution, but with the welfare of the entire Middle World.
Secondly, it is supposed to be held only once in each century. Consequently, those who participate in it have never seen it performed before, so
that it must be created entirely on the basis of the descriptions given in
several ancient manuscripts. It is thus the clearest possible example of the
process that I have termed "the sounding of the text." Thirdly, as with
most events in Bali, there is an interesting discrepancy between the ideal
and the real. Although the texts state that Eka Dasa Rudra should be held
punctually at the end of each Icaka century, it is not clear that the
ceremony had *ever* been performed until March of 1963, when it was held
at the wrong time, 16 years before the end of the cycle. The ceremony was
held again in 1979, which corresponds to the Icaka year 1900 and was thus
the correct date according to the ancient manuscripts. This second
performance of Eka Dasa Rudra involved nearly every Balinese in a
tremendous effort to revitalize the institutions of the classical civilization,
in the face of the disasters of the twentieth century and the intrusive

Figure 7.1. The temple of Besakih, site of the Eka Dasa Rudra ceremonies. The large building on the right is the orchestra pavilion.

presence of modern bureaucratic civilization. In this chapter, we will consider the ceremony of Eka Dasa Rudra as a supreme example of the power of the sounding of the texts to shape social reality.

We will begin by considering the texts that provided the foundation for the ceremony and the manner in which these texts were interpreted.

THE LOGIC OF THE CEREMONY

Rudra is an ancient Indian war god, probably pre-Vedic, whose name means "Howler" in Sanskrit. In Balinese Hindu-Buddhism, Rudra is identified as Siwa, the supreme deity, in his most terrible demonic form. Eka Dasa Rudra ("The Eleven Rudras") conceive of the god as divided into 11 shapes and distributed in space to pervade the entire macrocosm at the points of the compass and the center, the zenith, and the nadir. Eka Dasa Rudra, then, symbolically represents the chthonic or destructive powers at large in the Universe.

The ceremony Karya Taur Agung Eka Dasa Rudra ("Great Offering to the Eleven Rudras") is mentioned in several *lontar* texts, and it was these descriptions which provided the basis for holding the ceremony in 1963 and again in 1979. The *lontar* "Tutur Rogasenggara" states that Eka Dasa

Figure 7.2. One of the principal shrines at Besakih, decorated for the Eka Dasa Rudra rituals. The three pinnacles are shrines to the Hindu gods Brahma, Siwa, and Wisnu.

Rudra is the supreme "purification" ceremony (*buta yadnya*) and should be held when the last two digits of the Isaka year are zero; in other words, at the end of the century. According to the text, great changes will occur in both the macrocosm and the microcosm (*buana agung* and *buana alit*) at this time, and this ceremony will help to control the destructive power of change. This rationale is in accord with the general Balinese perspective on time, which we have examined in some detail in earlier chapters,

Figure 7.3. Statue of the god Rama from the epic poem Ramayana, standing guard at the gates to Besakih temple.

according to which everything in nature is perceived as being on a cycle of growth followed by decay. In this *lontar*, a 100-year cycle is attributed to the entire Middle World. Thus Eka Dasa Rudra is depicted as a kind of grand temple festival designed to ensure the prosperity of the entire Middle World, just as lesser temple festivals provide for the well-being of its constituent parts.

If Eka Dasa Rudra is to be a sort of ultimate temple festival to ensure the vitality of the Middle World for a 100-year period, a question arises as to which temple should hold the festival. For presumably only a temple with authority over the entire Middle World would be appropriate. This question is addressed in several *lontars*, all of which state that Eka Dasa Rudra must be held in the temple of Besakih (see Figure 7.1).

Besakih is one of Bali's most interesting temples (see Figures 7.2 and 7.3). It is now routinely described as Bali's "Mother Temple," the supreme temple of the island. But the actual history of the temple is rather more complex. Dr. Roeloef Goris, who was director of the archeological service on Bali for many years under both the Dutch and Indonesian administrations, conducted historical investigations on Besakih that were set forth in two articles: "De Poera Besakih, Bali's Rijkstempel" ("Bali's State Temple of Besakih") and "Een Plechtige Bede in een Eeuwenoud Heiligdon" ("A Solemn Prayer Spoken in an Ancient Sanctuary").[1] In these articles, Goris suggests that Besakih is older than Hindu-Buddhist civilization on Bali, that it was originally an ancient megalithic terraced sanctuary to the mountain god of Gunung Agung. Besakih is located on the slopes of Gunung Agung, Bali's largest volcano. According to Goris this sanctuary was appropriated by the lords of Gelgel as their ancestor shrine when they became the rulers of Bali around the fourteenth century.

> Following the success of the punitive force which had completely routed the Balinese ruler, viceroys were sent from [the Javanese kingdom of] Majapahit. One of the viceroys was Arya Kapakisan, whose grandson established himself in Gelgel about 1400. In countless chronicles and legends this first prince of Gelgel is closely associated with the Pura Besakih. There is no doubt that the princes of Gelgel transformed the prehistoric terraced sanctuary on the Gunung Agung into their own ancestral temple, making it the main official temple of the entire island over which they ruled with the title of Dewa Agung. The Pura Besakih continued to fulfill this function even when, centuries later, the princes of Gelgel transferred the seat of their dynasty to Klungkung.[2]

Besakih presently consists of a complex of approximately 170 shrines situated on a series of terraces. The central sanctuary is associated with the Gelgel/Klungkung dynasty, with its claim to supremacy over the entire island. An upper complex of shrines, to the west of the main sanctuary, is controlled by the former principality of Bangli, while a similar shrine on the upper west falls under the jurisdiction of the former princedom of Karangasem. The northern princedom of Buleleng was responsible for the upkeep of a northerly shrine, while the southerly principalities of Gianyar and Badung were responsible for two southerly shrines. Thus the location of the shrines corresponds roughly to the position of the princedoms that were connected to the central palace at Klungkung (see map). Goris describes Besakih as the royal dynastic temple of the rulers of Bali from about 1400 until the present. The actual situation is more complicated, however.

This arrangement does suggest the symbolism of a royal dynastic temple for the entire island. But the symmetry is broken by the absence of three major princedoms. According to Goris,

> Of the other regions formerly under the rule of the local princes, three, Tabanan, Mengwi and Jembrana, did not participate in the maintenance of the sanctuary on the Gunung Agung. [Note: as we have seen, according to the logic of Balinese temples, all groups belonging to a temple congregation must share in its maintenance.] Tabanan did not take part in the ceremonies at the sanctuary on the Gunung Agung, having its own mountain temple, the Pura Dasar on the Batu Kau, which may also have served as a mountain temple for [the princedom of] Mengwi. Although Jembrana now contributes towards the maintenance costs, formerly it did not do so, for it remained outside the kingdoms of both Gelgel and Klungkung.[3]

Thus in order for the Pura Besakih to become identified as the supreme temple of Bali, with authority over the entire Middle World, a major symbolic redefinition had to occur. The annual ritual cycle at Besakih normally involves 55 separate ceremonies conducted at various shrines by the groups associated with them. For example, once every 210 days, representatives from the Pasek Kayu Selem clan perform offerings to their ancestors at the shrine numbered 28. These ceremonies would not involve anyone else, except possibly temple priests attached to the whole temple complex. The most important annual ritual is the Bhatara Turun Kabeh ("The Gods Descend"), when the major gods are worshipped by the descendants of the rulers of nineteenth century Balinese courts, excluding Mengwi, Jembrana, and Buleleng.

For Besakih to play the role of the symbolic summit of all temple networks, that is the supreme temple and center of the middle World, the association of particular groups with the temple had to be deemphasized in favor of a symbolic association with all Balinese. To be included in the ceremonies, the former courts of Tabanan, Mengwi, and Jembrana had to be given some responsibilities for preparations for the Eka Dasa Rudra. More importantly, *all* major temple networks had to be mobilized and given specific tasks. In the absence of direct instructions from the *lontar* texts, this symbolic rearrangement was conducted according to the general logic of Balinese temples. Representatives from every major institutional group were given responsibility to contribute specific offerings, labor, or sums of money, and in this way all major temple networks were incorporated into the temple congregation of Besakih. In the preparations for the 1979 celebration of Eka Desa Rudra, every Balinese village, descent group, farmer's association, and former court was asked to contribute. Thus a villager might help with the preparations for Eka Dasa Rudra once as a member of his village (*desa*), another time as a member of an irrigation society (*subak*), and again as a member of a descent group (*soroh*).

In this way, Besakih could become, for the first time in its history, as far as we know, supreme over all the 20,000 temples of Bali. However, the first attempt to achieve this marshalling of the whole of Balinese civilization was not entirely successful.

EKA DASA RUDRA IN 1963

Since the purpose of Eka Dasa Rudra is to regulate the forces of decay at the end of a century, transforming them into power for new growth, it seems paradoxical that the ceremony should have been held in 1963, when the century had yet another 16 years to run. The high priests who decided to hold the ceremony at that time based their decision on a single *lontar* text, the "Chronicle of King Jayakasunu." The relevant passages from this text are translated below.

> Jayakasunu was a prince who, before allowing himself to become king of Bali, decided to perform yoga and meditation in order to discover why all previous kings died before their reigns had lasted a year. Accordingly Jayakasunu retreated to a place called Gandamayu. [In a book published by the committee which organized Eka Dasa Rudra in 1979, the comment is made that "According to old tales, Gandamayu is located in the area of the present Temple of Besakih."] There, Jayakasunu received advice from the Goddess Durga; an incarnation of the suprme god Siwa:
>
>> Hai Jayakasunu, the reason why every ruler of Bali lives but a short life, dying after only reigning for one year, and the reason why there are plagues and pestilence of many kinds throughout the realm, is because the Six Great Temples are left in ruins, and ceremonies are not being carried out every year at Besakih Temple. Whenever there are great misfortunes, such as the land becoming innundated by the waters

of the sea, or a rain of burning ashes, or darkness in the daytime, then should be held the Eka Dasa Rudra at Besakih. Also there should be held Tawur [chthonic] sacrifices at the sea in the sixth, seventh or eighth month, in order to return the plagues of mice and sickness, all of the plagues which infect the villages and sawah-fields, because they all come from the sea.

In the ninth Icaka month, it is appropriate to call the gods down to go to the seaside in the melelasti ceremony. On the date of the Ninth Dark Moon it is necessary to hold the Demon offerings Pancasanak and "Stillness" [Nyunia Desa].

If these things are not done properly, all of them, there will be endless disasters, earthquakes, the age of men will be very short, and they will not cease to meet misfortunes, the creations of men will become strange. Everything will be inverted, good men will be bad and bad men good.

If the ruler wishes to prevent these things so that conditions become normal, he must hold the Eka Dasa Rudra at Besakih. If everything I have described to you is well done, the Brahmans will reach the highest dharma, the Wesyas and Rulers [Satriya] will perform their dharma well, also the Sudras, and the binding of society will again be strong. (my translation)

The passage in the text which states that Eka Dasa Rudra should be held whenever a great misfortune occurs provided the basis for the decision to hold the ceremony in March of 1963, at the end of the Icaka year. At that time Bali was in a state of political and economic turmoil. It was felt by many that the disasters of the twentieth century—the bloody slaughter of the great courts, the Dutch and Japanese occupations, the struggle for independence, and the widespread corruption and economic decay of the post-independence period—warranted holding the Eka Dasa Rudra before the century's end. But the decision was quickly taken out of the hands of the Balinese religious authorities. President Sukarno was about to launch his "New Order" for Indonesia, and seized on the Balinese ceremony as a splendid symbol with which to mark a new beginning. Sukarno personally invited representatives from the world tourist industry, in the form of the Pacific Area Travel Agents (PATA), to hold their annual meetings in Bali at the time of the festival. Debate among Balinese religious scholars over whether to initiate the Eka Dasa Rudra so far ahead of the century's end was still continuing when Sukarno announced that he would arrive with a party of official guests, and the PATA delegates, to personally attend the ceremonies.

The events which followed are often compared by Balinese literati to one of the grim royal tragedies of Balinese legendary histories, with Sukarno cast in the role of over-proud monarch. The story is well summarized by Willard Hanna.

The priests were constrained to defer to official ukase. The Eka Dasa Rudra was scheduled to begin on March 8 and to continue for approximately one month as a sort of command performance for President Sukarno and his state guests.

On February 18, just as the preparations at Besakih were getting well under way with the construction of a special archway honoring President Sukarno and other works of ornamentation at the temple site, Mt. Agung suddenly began to emit smoke and ash, and occasional earth tremors could be clearly felt. In the course of the next several weeks volcanic activities continued and intensified. Again the religious authorities argued for reconsideration; again they were overruled. On March 8, therefore, although swirls of smoke and a dusting of volcanic ash were perceptible in the immediate Besakih area, the ceremonies began. But the priests were fearful of profanation of the sanctuary; the crowds apprehensive rather than festive; Sukarno himself failed to show up. The Eka Dasa Rudra, which started as a disappointment, turned into a disaster.

On March 12, while the ceremonies still continued, Mt. Agung began to throw out mud and rock. By March 17 great rivers of molten lava were pouring down the mountainside. Flames leaped higher and higher into the sky; smoke and volcanic ash blotted out the sun and darkened the countryside. The Besakih temple complex, situated on a sharp ridge and bracketed by deep valleys through which the lava flowed, escaped the main line of destruction. But it was covered deep in hot ash; the palm fibre thatch of the shrines was set ablaze, as were some of the wooden superstructures. The main sanctuaries themselves were miraculously spared, but the very first casualty was the ornamental gateway built to honor Sukarno. By then not only Bali but the whole of the nation was aware that Mt. Agung had terminated the ceremonies which Sukarno had ordered. Javanese as well as Balinese interpreted this as a divine judgement on the Sukarno regime. Not only the island of Bali, but the eastern end of Java was darkened at midday by dense clouds of smoke and ash such as no one could remember ever having experienced before.[4]

EKA DASA RUDRA IN 1979

The remaining years of the Icaka century brought further disasters, and extremely rapid social changes, tending in the minds of many Balinese to confirm the original postulate on which Eka Dasa Rudra was based, that the end of a century is the time when the forces of decay are strongest. Clearly, the further survival of Balinese civilization depended on bringing those forces under control. Sukarno's regime tottered, and ultimately collapsed in 1965. In the aftermath of the bloody coup, thousands of Balinese died in power struggles between rival parties and factions, which continued for months.

A few years later, before Bali had fully recovered from the aftermath of the 1963 Eka Dasa Rudra, strange new forces were introduced into Balinese life. Eka Dasa Rudra had hardly been a successful tourist attraction, but nonetheless Sukarno's plans for transforming Bali into a major center of tourism were spectacularly fulfilled. An international airport opened in 1969, and 30,000 tourists visited Bali in that year. In 1979 a third of a million tourists arrived in the space of a single calendar year. Since by then the total population of Bali was only 2¼ million, the influx of such vast numbers of foreign visitors put major strains on Balinese hospitality. Often, Balinese found it almost impossible to complete temple ceremonies, or even personal ceremonies such as weddings and funerals, because of the pressure of uninvited guests.

In a more subtle, but in some ways more threatening, manner, the advanced Western technology which the tourists brought with them (the hotels, buses, cameras, jet aircraft, yachts, and even helicopters) confronted the Balinese with a more powerful, technologically superior form of civilization. Most tourists were lodged in several large hotel complexes on the south coast. From these fortresses buses would set forth each morning in search of interesting events. At any moment, they might swoop down on a gathering of Balinese conducting the cremation of a relative, rehearsing for a performance, or even taking a bath in a grotto. In the space of ten years, Bali had been transformed into something uncomfortably close to a wild animal park. As the number of tourists, buses, and hotels swelled, more and more Balinese found themselves the objects of these photographic safaris.

And so, as the end of the Icaka century approached, there does not seem to have been any debate as to whether or not to hold the Eka Dasa Rudra ceremony. The forces of change and decay were clearly very powerful and obviously capable of overwhelming Balinese civilization if not brought under control. The meaning of the Eka Dasa Rudra ceremony for the Balinese in 1979 was captured in an interesting fashion in a television broadcast by an official of the Department of Religion, a religious scholar, several weeks before the climax of the ceremonies. In the preceding year, television sets had been set up in many Balinese villages, and a broadcast station had been constructed on the island. The following is a transcript of this speech, which was taped and broadcast several times in the closing weeks before Eka Dasa Rudra:

> To those honored persons who are about to watch this broadcast, peace
> and welcome unto you. Now I wish to provide an explanation for
> those who may hear my words of the ceremony we are performing,
> Eka Dasa Rudra. This explanation is based on the information pro-

vided by learned persons and also upon the knowledge of the sacred *lontar* manuscripts. The *lontar* manuscripts, which we have consulted, include Sundari Gamo, Asta Kosala Bumi, and many others. Each year at the time of the changing of the Isaka year, that is at the turning of the Ninth Dark Moon, it is appropriate to hold the Tawur sacrifices, or offerings. The Tawur sacrifices are performed for the Gods of the Underworld but they are intended to receive the blessings of the Great God, Sanghyang Widi Wasa, so the whole world can be cleansed and the welfare of the world's people be maintained. It is necessary to hold this type of ceremony once each year. Furthermore, at the close or ending of each five year cycle, for example in the Icsaka Year 1880 because the cycle is longer, the ceremony is raised to a greater level of completeness or perfection. This is called Pancha Wali Krama. At the close of a ten year cycle, an even higher level ceremony is performed. At the close of 10 ten year cycles, there is the greatest of all cycles, and its closing requires that the greatest of Tawur sacrifices be performed, called Eka Dasa Rudra. This is the ceremony which is to be performed now. Now I, for my part, propose a question. Why must it be that this ceremony be held at the close of 10 ten year cycles?

Followers of the Dharma, this is the explanation which is given us by those who are learned in these matters. Every process of trans-formation, whether in the microcosmos or Buana Alit, or the macro-cosmos, the universe called Buana Agung, brings changes. Growing from a child into an adult brings changes. Education from lower school to university brings many changes in one's experience and under-standing. But change must happen in the proper order, or it is dan-gerous. In order to control change, this ceremony must take place. Uncontrolled change can destroy peace like the fire of Agni, which is dangerous only when it is out of control. These are, in brief, the motivations behind the ceremony Eka Dasa Rudra, which we are about to hold. This completes my task of explanation for television. "Om, Santi, Santi, Santi, May there be no hindrance."[5] (my translation)

THE RITUAL SEQUENCE

The performance of Eka Dasa Rudra in 1979 was the largest and most complex Balinese temple festival of the twentieth century, and perhaps of all time. Literally tons of intricate offerings were created for presentation to the Rudras and the gods. In the central temple area (the Pura Penataran Agung), most of the offerings were renewed each day. The sequence of ceremonies continued for weeks and occupied all of the major priests of Bali. But since the *lontar* texts that mention the Eka Dasa Rudra provide only a general outline of the major ceremonies, innumerable rituals had to be spontaneously invented. The logic that governed these improvisations was quite simple: several *lontars* state explicitly that Eka Dasa Rudra is the supreme ritual of one of the major groups of Balinese ritual, of which there are five in all. These five groups are

1. Manusia Yadnya: initiation rituals (from birth rituals to marriage)
2. Resi Yadnya: consecration ceremonies for priests
3. Pitra Yadnya: ceremonies for the deceased and offerings to the ancestors
4. Dewa Yadnya: ceremonies of worship for the gods
5. Buta Yadnya: exorcistic rituals, to appease the powers of the nether-world

The ceremonies of Buta Yadnya are offerings to the demonic powers. For Eka Dasa Rudra, these offerings were simply made more complete and comprehensive than ever before, but conforming to the standard patterns of *buta* (demon) offerings. It is easy to be misled by the apparent naiveté of the concept of "demon offerings." Balinese religion is a sophisticated blend of Hinduism, Buddhism, and indigenous beliefs, and the ceremonies of Buta Yadnya are not simple-minded offerings of appeasement to slavering devils. All Balinese "demons" may take form either in the outer world (*buana agung*) or the world of the self, the microcosmos (*buana alit*). Demons (*buta*) may be viewed from many perspectives. A strong Buddhist element in Balinese religion suggests that demons are essentially psychological projections, but differs from Western psychology in insisting that "demonic" forces are part of the intrinsic constitution of inner and outer reality. The demons, according to this interpretation, are simply the raw elements from which the higher realities of consciousness and the world are created. *Buta*, which is usually glossed as "demon," actually means "element." The ceremonies of Buta Yadnya always involve sacrifices dramatizing the processes of death, decomposition, and rebirth. Eka Dasa Rudra, which as supreme Buta Yadnya is concerned with the elements of the entire Middle World, was felt to require the sacrifice of representatives of every species of animal. Each creature would be killed and its body divided into 102 pieces, representing the 102 elements of which the Middle World is composed. These elements would then be placed in the shrines of the eleven Rudras, the supreme elements (*buta*). Symbolically, the Middle World is decomposed into its constituent elements (or demons, *buta*) at the end of a cycle, to prepare for a new cycle of growth. The 102 elements are dissolved through the sacrificial death of each "higher" creature.

Several *lontars* explicitly mention particular animals required for the sacrifice. The manuscript *Dangdang Bang Bungalan*, for example, states that Eka Dasa Rudra, as the supreme ceremony in the Buta Yadnya cycle, requires the sacrifice of 28 water buffalo. Collectively, the texts were taken to imply that representatives of all known species should be sacrificed. An elephant was sought but ultimately spared; however pieces of elephant and rhinoceros skin were obtained and used.

The "Great Offering" of these sacrifices was conducted according to the instructions contained in the manuscript *Pawilangan Indik Puja Ring Pura Besakih* (*Ceremonies of Worship at the Temple of Besakih*), which described a great ceremonial enclosure in the shape of a *mandala*, or map of the universe, to be constructed at the gates of the main temple. There were 11 shrines created at the 8 points of the compass and the zenith, center, and nadir, representing the locations of the 11 Rudras. According to Balinese cosmology, this shape reflects the structure of both the macrocosmos and the microcosmos.

The sacrifices and offerings were piled before each of these shrines, representing the regrouping of the basic elements (*buta*) around the 11 poles of the universe. At the instant the century turned (according to our calendar, at noon on March 28, 1979), teams of high priests attempted to realign these constituent elements of the Middle World, so that the process of decomposition would be transformed into growth. This transformation was symbolically portrayed in two drawings placed in the center of the enclosure: The first showed the god Siwa springing out of the demon Kala, the second showed the goddess Uma springing out of the demoness Durga. The meaning of this symbolic transformation is complex and profound. On the one hand, the Rudras were conceived of as tangible beings that high priests might be able to glimpse. President Suharto of Indonesia was invited to attend the ceremony, but was asked not to arrive in his helicopter, for fear its passage might annoy the descending demons. But on the other hand, Balinese priests and scholars continually emphasized that the process of dissolution and realignment of elements should occur simultaneously in the outer world and the inner world of the self. The *performance* of Eka Dasa Rudra should compel participants to confront the decaying elements of their own being, and through their participation in the ceremony regain the control of their elemental being necessary to begin the new cycle of history in a growth phase.

A parallel was drawn between the animal sacrifices and the human worshippers. Before its death, the soul of each creature was set free in a special ritual, soon to seek rebirth in a Middle World purified and improved by the Eka Dasa Rudra sacrifices. The soul is thus considered to be independent of the elements that make up its physical body (*buta*). Without the necessity of leaving its body, the soul of each person was asked to realign the elements of its own base nature, to regain control over its own destructive tendencies.

CONCLUSION: THE PERFORMANCE OF EKA DASA RUDRA

As we have seen in earlier chapters, the function of Balinese temple festivals is to bring together all of the forces at work in the life of an institution, so that they may reach whatever accommodations are necessary in order for the institution to prosper through another cycle of its existence. In a sense, Eka Dasa Rudra represented the same process on a far more ambitious scale. The temple of Besakih had to be redefined as the symbolic summit of all temple networks, with authority over the activities of the entire Middle World. According to the logic of Balinese temple festivals, this could be done only by including representatives from all major institutional systems of Bali in the preparations at Besakih.

The ceremony of Eka Dasa Rudra was the quintessential sounding of the text, transforming a few lines of prose from several ancient manuscripts into a world-shaping reality. The *performance* of Eka Dasa Rudra created an interpretive framework with which to view the major events of the twentieth century from the perspective of classical Balinese civilization. Eka Dasa Rudra dramatically established a framework: there is a Middle World, whose center is at Besakih, which is subject to a 100-year cycle of growth and decay, and the course of events on this macrolevel may be affected in the same way that they are dealt with on the microlevel, with temple performances.

The overt purpose of the ceremony was to confront the forces that threatened the dissolution of the Middle World. But these forces (the Rudras) and the Middle World itself were given many interpretations. The *performance* of Eka Dasa Rudra created a kaleidoscopic rearrangement of many levels of reality and interpretation, in accordance with what I termed in Chapter 4 the "reflexive aesthetics" of the Balinese. Thus the Middle World came to stand for the visible world, the macrocosm, the island of Bali, and perhaps most fundamentally, Balinese civilization. The Rudras in turn were variously depicted as tangible beings that could get caught in a helicopter's whirling blades, as the constituent elements of the outer universe, as personifications of the forces of decay, as a psychological tendency inside each person, and as the specific threats to Balinese classical civilization that have become manifest in this century.

The sounding of the texts of Eka Dasa Rudra drew all these themes and issues together, compelling the Balinese to see themselves as citizens of a Middle World whose continued welfare depends on their reactions to the forces of change.

Conclusion:
Vehicles of the
Imagination

The first written texts reached Bali from the Indic world, sometime in the second half of the first millenium A.D. From the standpoint of their significance for the Balinese, it does not matter greatly whether they were brought more or less directly from India, or via some Indicized Southeast Asian kingdom. We shall probably never know whether the first texts arrived in the hands of traders, ambassadors, mendicant monks, or Balinese emissaries returning from a visit to a foreign court, but one suspects that in the course of time, probably all of these possibilities were realized. By the ninth century A.D., Balinese rulers were composing texts of their own in two languages, Sanskrit and Old Balinese, the former addressed to the Indic world and the latter to the king's subjects. In these inscriptions, we can trace the efforts of Balinese rulers to appropriate for themselves the new models of kingship and society conveyed by the Indic texts.

We cannot know precisely which texts were being held up to the royal courts as models during this formative period, but the inscriptions of the tenth and eleventh centuries mention a wide variety of Hindu and Buddhist sects, each of which must have possessed its own texts. No single sect appears to have prevailed over the others, so it seems more accurate to speak of "Hindu-Buddhist" or simply "Indic" models, rather than those of any single Hindu or Buddhist tradition. Consider, for example, the eleventh century monarch Anak Wungcu. In his own inscriptions he is referred to as an incarnation of the Preserver of the World, the god Wiṣnu, which suggests that he adhered to Vaiṣnavite Hinduism. But his chief advisers included the heads of Buddhist and Saivite Hindu monasteries, and he supported many royal hermits and sects (the cults of Ganesha and Surya are specifically mentioned). Finally, the inscriptions record his support for several large monastic communities, the remains of some of which are still visible in the hills around Gunung Kawi.

The influence of the inhabitants of these monastaries was not confined to the royal courts. An inscription of 1073 A.D. describes Balinese society as being divided into the four castes of the Varna system (Brahmana, Ksatriya, Waisya, and Sudra) and the slaves (hulun). Regardless of the degree to which society actually conformed to this model, the inscription itself is significant as evidence of the ruler's desire to impose Indic models on society at large, as well as on his court. Meanwhile, many inscriptions record in great detail the varied ways in which villagers were directed to help support the monks, including direct taxes, labor, and defense. Monks might live in monasteries, at court, alone in hermitages or as mendicants, or even in villages. But all of them relied on villagers for part or all of their support.

The inscriptions unfortunately—but unsurprisingly—do not mention specifically the "reading clubs" (sekehe bebasan) that exist today, nor do they refer to monks reading texts or sermons to the villagers. But they do describe in extraordinary detail the intertwining networks of performing artists, based in courts, villages, monasteries, and as independent "roving" troupes, who played a role in village affairs of sufficient importance to warrant extensive attention in the royal proclamations. I draw attention in particular to the artists or "entertainers" (bhandagina), who were directly under the control of the "head of the dharma [religious foundation]," and to the royal troupes. Through the sanctioned performances of these artists, the sounding of the texts was carried beyond the royal palaces and monasteries into the villages and countryside. For while it seems unlikely—and indeed, we cannot know—that the ability to read had spread very far among the villagers, clearly, performing the texts had the power to convey their meaning with directness and immediacy.

Many of these performances must have occurred in conjunction with temple festivals. The inscriptions make frequent reference to temples and temple taxes and occasional specific reference to performances held in temple rituals. One of the very earliest inscriptions, for example (Trunyan B. 1, 911 A.D.), directs the inhabitants of the hamlet of Air Rawang, to the east of Lake Batur, to participate in the temple festivals for the god Bhatara Da Tonta. The god's statue is to be bathed, coated with yellow oils, and adorned with jeweled finger and ear rings. These rituals, along with various purification ceremonies, are to be held in the temple in the month of Bhadrawada (August). Inscriptions like this testify to the antiquity of the village temple system, with its calendrical rituals and performances. Other inscriptions confirm the interest of both the ruler and religious authorities in village temples. Villagers are empowered, in edicts from the tenth century onward, to build new temples, to accept monks as village residents, to support priests, to incorporate *meru* roofs (echoing Hindu/ Buddhist cosmology) on village temples, and to create hermitages (*pertapaan*) and resting places for religious travelers.

In this way, the island became populated with Brahmans and *bhikkus*, princes and princesses, gods and goddesses, and poets and performers. Palaces, temples, and monasteries were built and decorated with images of the Indic gods and heroes. Under the patronage of the kings, Hindu and Buddhist holy men were incorporated into village affairs, and with the assistance of poets and artists, brought the worlds of Indic mythology into the lives of the villagers. And in the performances held in temples, courts, and monasteries, the civilization of the Middle World took form. The kings themselves became incarnations of the Hindu high gods, their tombs became temples, and their histories merged into the Hindu myths and legends. Eventually the monasteries were abandoned, but the priests and rituals, and above all the libraries, survived.

We can only speculate as to the reasons for the decline of monasticism, which appears to have been so important in the early phases of Balinese civilization, and as to the evolution of the temple system that in some sense took its place. But when historical ethnographic evidence became available, in the nineteenth century, Bali had developed into a civilization of temples. It seems plausible to claim that the use of temples as organizational systems was carried further in Bali than in any other Asian society, although in the Kandyan and Angkorean kingdoms, particularly, temples seem to have played an important economic and social role. But in Bali, thousands of temples were packed into Lilliputian kingdoms, each temple dedicated to the activities of some particular group. Temples developed into complex and sophisticated—if somewhat unwieldy—institutional networks controlling everything from village affairs to rice agriculture and kinship organization.

Much that is unique about Balinese culture derives from the fact that these temples play a dual role. In one sense, they actively manage collective affairs in ways that we would not ordinarily associate with the concept of "temples." The functions of Balinese temples extend far beyond those we would describe as "religious." Temple "activations" (*odalan*)—a uniquely Balinese phenomenon—are occasions for all of the people concerned with some institution (a village, ward, descent group, farmer's association, kingdom, etc.) to gather together to chart their collective course. Water temples literally—and very effectively—organize the schedule of irrigation and farming activities connected with wet-rice cultivation. Historically, the inscriptions show how the old villages-as-territorial-units (*wanua*, a Malayo-Polynesian word for village used in the early inscriptions) were supplanted by the concept of villages-as-temple-clusters (*desa*, a Sanskrit word meaning "state," which eventually replaced the term *wanua* altogether). Today, even banks and the post office have their own temples, whose activations mark the anniversaries of their construction.

In addition to this "institutional" function, temples possess a transcendant function based on their role in Balinese cosmology. According to this cosmology, human activities can never be exclusively secular because they occur in cycles or phases of growth and decline that do not really begin or end in the human (Middle) world. Instead, they lead into the other worlds of the gods, demons, and ancestors, all of whom are enmeshed in the events of the Middle World. Temple activations provide an opportunity to try to achieve the necessary harmony among these diverse and potentially conflicting interests—without which any merely human project will assuredly fail. Temples are bridges between the three worlds.

From an anthropological perspective, temples are theaters where the arts portray the denizens of the three worlds and by sounding the texts induce the temple congregations to view themselves in the context of this cosmology. Because of the dual nature of temples—organizing the affairs of daily life and at the same time reflecting that life in the mirror of the Indic texts—the social order is perceived to be in a permanent state of imperfection, or incompleteness. Discrepancies between the ideal and the real social worlds are constantly highlighted in temple performances; but not, however, simply to chastise the congregation, rather, to nudge them into a more perfect realization of the ideals celebrated by the sounding of the texts.

It is in this context that it makes sense to think of Balinese civilization as an artistic creation, the product of the sounding of the texts. In broad terms, civilization may be defined as a complex institutional system that organizes social life through ties that extend beyond kinship. In Bali, such an organizational system was created through intricate networks of thousands of temples. The very existence of these temples is explainable only in terms of their relationship to the performing arts on the one hand and to Balinese cosmology on the other. The relationship among these elements—temples, texts, performances, and cosmology—is essentially circular: temples exist to hold festivals, where they are activated by the performing arts, whose function is to sound the texts of Balinese cosmology, which establish a world view in which temples are essential to the continued functioning of the Middle World.

The statistical analysis in Chapter 3 strongly supports this analysis, although it remains possible that an alternative theory might be devised that would also fit the statistical picture. Temples and art groups are nearly perfectly correlated, and they are clustered in the areas where Indic civilization is oldest, if the archaeological picture is accurate. These are precisely the areas where the temple system achieved its greatest organizational triumph: an extraordinarily sensitive system for organizing wet-rice cultivation that realized optimal productivity with minimal ecological disturbance. The rice terraces and water temples of Bali became one of the most successful productive systems ever created by any society. In those regions, temples proliferated and temple activations became correspondingly more frequent, more artists were supported and more performances were held, the sounding of the texts became more pervasive, and the whole of social life came closer to the ideals celebrated by the sounding of the texts in the temple festivals.

The villages of the Bali Aga play an interesting role in this analysis because they seem at once to confirm it and at the same time to show its limitations. On the one hand, they are, quite simply, the villages where the texts are not sounded: there are no libraries, reading clubs, or *bebali* performances, and languages other than Balinese are virtually unknown. Therefore, these villages remain largely aloof from the ongoing struggles to force social life into some kind of conformity with the models presented by the texts. The institutions and rituals of caste do not exist. Village temples, although they bear a superficial resemblance to those of the wet-rice heartlands, actually fulfill very different functions, for they do not link the villagers to institutions that transcend the boundaries of the village.

But on the other hand, there is no apparent discrepancy in these villages between the ideal models celebrated in temple festivals and the reality of social life. Where "heartland" temple performances focus on discrepancies between the real and the ideal, Bali Aga performances portray a simple model of unchanging order based on the regularity of temporal changes, which does indeed appear to mirror the structure of all important village institutions. But do the arts create, or merely reflect, this model of temporal order? And is the mirror image a true reflection of the social world, or is it also merely a desired approximation? Let us hope that answers to these questions may be found while traditional Bali Aga villages still exist, because in the past decade many of them have been strongly affected by various aspects of "modernization."

But as Eka Dasa Rudra demonstrated, the civilization of the Middle World is still very much alive and will remain so for as long as the texts continue to be sounded in the temples. The fragile strength of this tradition is beautifully illustrated by a discovery made in 1935 by a Dutch archaeologist, Dr. W. F. Stutterheim, when he was conducting the first archaeological survey of Bali. In his report, Stutterheim describes an incident that occurred while he was investigating the tenth century shrines clustered around the sacred spring of Tirtha Empul.

> Exploring the vicinity, I found a short distance away, in a village called Manukaya, a much weather-worn inscription on a stone. None of the Balinese could decipher the old engraved letters, nor were the contents of the inscription known to anyone. The stone stood there, as every villager of Manukaya knew it from childhood, wrapped in a white cloth and provided with the regular offerings. I was told, however, that on the fourth month of every year, at full moon, this stone (which is also said to have fallen from the sky) is carried to the holy waters of Tirtha Empul and bathed therein—much to the detriment of the stone, by the way, which is a big slab of soft grey tufa covered as usual with a thin layer of cement.
>
> Deciphering the inscription, I found that it was none other than the charter of Tirtha Empul's foundation, made in the fourth month, at full-moon day, in the year 962 A.D. Thus the people have kept alive the connection between stone and watering-place for almost 1,000 years, and have always celebrated its anniversary on the correct date, but of the true meaning of this connection every recollection was lost.[1]

The inscription and the sacred pools were created by Sang Ratu Cri Candra Bhaya Singha Warmadeva, one of the earliest known Balinese kings.

Notes

ABBREVIATIONS

AA	*American Anthropologist*
BEFEO	*Bulletin d l'Ecole Francaise d'Extreme Orient,* Hanoi/Paris
BKI	*Bijdragen tot de Taal-, Land-, en Volkenkunde (van Nederlandsch-Indie),* published by the Koninklijk Instituut voor Taal-, Land-, en Volkenkunde, Leiden, The Netherlands
D	*Djawa*: Tijdschrift van het Java-Instituut, Jogjakarta, Java
I	*Indonesie*: (Tweemaandelijks) tijdschrift gewijd aan het Indonesisch cultuurgebied
MM	*Mensch en Maatshappij,* Amsterdam
TBG	*Tijdschrift voor Indische Taal-, Land-, en Volkenkunde,* uitgegeven door het (Koninklijk) Bataviaasch Genootschap van Kunsten en Wetenschappen, The Hague
TNI	*Tijdschrift voor Nederlandsch Indie*
UNUD	Universitas Udayana Publication Series, Denpasar, Bali
VBG	*Verhandelingen van het (Koninklijk) Bataviaansch Genootschap van Kunsten en Wetenschappen,* The Hague
VIG	*Verslag der Algemeene Verhandelingen van het Indische Genootschap*

CHAPTER 1

1. Margaret Mead, "The Arts in Bali", originally published in The Yale Review, XXX, No. 2 (December 1940), pp. 335–347; reprinted in Jane Belo, (Ed.), *Introduction to Traditional Balinese Culture*, Columbia University Press, 1970, p. 333.

2. Geoffrey Gorer, *Bali and Angkor, or Looking at Life and Death*. London: M. Joseph Ltd., 1936.

3. Antonin Artaud, *The Theater and Its Double*. New York: Grove Press, 1958.

4. Jane Belo, *Introduction to Traditional Balinese Culture*, op. cit., pp. xii–xiii.

5. *Ibid.*, p. xiii.

6. Arthur Waley, Preface to B. De Zoete and W. Spies, *Dance and Drama in Bali*. London: Faber and Faber, 1938, p. xix.

7. Mead, *op. cit.*, p. 334.

8. Clifford Geertz, Negara: *The Theatre State in Nineteenth Century Bali*. Princeton: Princeton University Press, 1980, pp. 19–20.

9. *Ibid.*, p. 13.

10. *Ibid.*, p. 14.

11. *Ibid.*, p. 125.

12. *Ibid.*, p. 13.

13. *Ibid.*, p. 123.

14. Paul Oskar Kristeller, "The Modern System of the Arts", in *Renaissance Thought II*. New York: Harper and Row, 1965, p. 226.

15. Charles Trinkaus, *In Our Image and Likeness: Humanity and Divinity in Italian Humanist Thought*, Vol. 2. Chicago: University of Chicago Press, 1970, p. 684.

16. Kristeller, *op. cit.*, p. 166.

17. *Ibid.*, p. 176.

18. *Ibid.*, p. 196.

19. *Ibid.*, p. 203.

20. *Ibid.*, p. 214.

21. *Ibid.*, p. 220.

22. Immanuel Kant, *Kritik der Reinen Vernunft, Transzendentale Aesthetik # 1*, Cassirer (Ed.), 3., Berlin, 1923, 56 pp.

23. Jacques Maquet, *Introduction to Aesthetic Anthropology*, McCaleb Module in Anthropology, New York: Addison-Wesley, 1971, pp. 9–14.

24. *Ibid.*, p. 14.

25. *Ibid.*, p. 6.

26. *Ibid.*, p. 7.

27. Quoted in Marshall Sahlins, *Culture and Practical Reason*, Chicago: University of Chicago Press, 1977, p. 65. See Franz Boas, Introduction to *Handbook of North American Indian Languages*, Preston Holder (Ed.). Lincoln: University of Nebraska Press, 1966, p. 14.

28. George Stocking, *Race, Language and Culture*. New York: Free Press, 1968, p. 159.

29. Marshall Sahlins, *Culture and Practical Reason, op. cit.*, p. viii.

CHAPTER 2

1. I. W. Mabbett, "The 'Indianization' of Southeast Asia: Reflections on the Prehistoric Sources," *Journal of Southeast Asian Studies*, Vol. VIII, No. 1, 1977; and "Reflections on the Historical Sources," *Journal of Southeast Asian Studies*, Vol. VIII, No. 2, 1977.

2. Paul Wheatley, "Satyantra in Suvarnadvipa", in Sabloff and C. C. Lamberg-Karlovsky (Eds.), *Ancient Civilization and Trade*. Albuquerque, New Mexico: University of New Mexico

Press, 1975. pp. 227–284; and Ken Hall, "The 'Indianization' of Funan": An Economic History of Southeast Asia's First State, *Journal of Southeast Asian Studies*, Fall 1981.

3. See note 2.

4. R. C. Majumdar, *Hindu Colonies in the Far East*, Calcutta, 1944/1963, p. 23.

5. J. C. van Leur, "On Early Asian Trade", in *Indonesian Trade and Society*, W. van Hoeve, The Hague and Bandung, 1955, p. 98.

6. For recent interviews on this topic, see Mabbett (*op. cit.*) and Ken Hall (*op. cit.*).

7. Hirananda Sastri, *Nalanda and Its Epigraphic Material*. Memoirs of the Archaeology Survey of India, No. 66. Calcutta: Government of India Press, 1942, pp. 101–102.

8. *Ibid.*, p. 119.

9. *Ibid.*, p. 15.

10. See S. N. Sen, *A Bibliography of Sanskrit Works in Astronomy and Mathematics*. Calcutta: National Institute of Science of India, 1966. An excellent summary of Indian achievements in these fields is provided by H. J. J. Winter, who concludes, "Hindu Mathematics is undoubtedly the finest intellectual achievement of the subcontinent in medieval times." (H. J. J. Winter, Science, in A. L. Basham (Ed.), *A Cultural History of India*. Oxford: Clarendon Press, 1975, pp. 141–162.

11. Winter, op. cit., p. 157.

12. Bernard-Phillipe Groslier, *Angkor Hommes et Pierres*. Paris: Arthand, 1956, p. 11.

13. Robert Heine-Geldern, "Conceptions of State and Kingship in Southeast Asia," *The Far Eastern Quarterly*, Vol. II, 1942, pp. 17–18.

14. Quoted from Paul Mus's transcription in Paul Wheatley, *The Pivot of the Four Quarters*, Chicago: Aldine, 1971, p. 437; note 81, p. 465; note 116, p. 469.

15. Wheatley, *ibid.*, p. 437.

16. *Ibid.*, p. 437.

17. See Georges Coedes, "La stele du Prah Khan d'Ankor", BEFEO, Vol. 41, 1941, stanzas XLIV–CLXV.

18. Wheatley, *op. cit.*, p. 265.

19. For a recent theoretical discussion of divine kingship in both the Hindu and Buddhist traditions, see S. J. Tambiah, *World Conqueror and World Renouncer*. Cambridge: Cambridge University Press, 1976, Chapters 2–4. Early formulations are provided by Heine-Geldern (*op. cit.*) and Georges Coedes, *Les Etats Hindouises d'Indochine et d'Indonesia* Paris, 1964, rev. ed., (translated as *The Indianized States of Southeast Asia*, Honolulu: East-West Center Press, 1968). Interesting essays and bibliographic references are provided by K. R. Hall and J. K. Whitmore (Eds.), *Explorations in Early Southeast Asian History: The Origins of Southeast Asian Statecraft*. Ann Arbor: Michigan Papers on South and Southeast Asian Studies, 1976.

20. The term "Late Formative" derives from Julian Steward's chronological framework for the development of states from a comparative perspective (Julian Steward, *Theory of Culture Change*. Chicago: University of Illinois Press, 1955, pp. 178–210). For recent studies utilizing this framework, see essays in H. J. M. Claessen and P. Skalnik (Eds.), *The Early State*. Mouton: The Hague, 1978.

21. See R. A. Blust, "Austronesian Culture History: Some linguistic inferences and their relation to the archaeological record," *World Archaeology* 8.1, 1976, pp. 19–43; and "Early Austronesian Social Organization: The evidence of language," *Current Anthropology* 21.2, 1980. For the controversy on early iron, etc., see the comments following the latter article.

22. On Dong-Son culture, see H. R. van Heekeren, *The Bronze-Iron Age of Indonesia*. Verhandelingen van het Koningklijk Institut, Deel XXII, 's-Gravenhage, M. Nijhoff, 1958, Chapter 4. For a recent appraisal, see R. P. Soejono, "The History of Prehistoric Research in Indonesia up to 1950," *Asian Perspectives* XII, 1969, pp. 69–91, and the sources listed in note 23 (below).

23. Sources on megalithic culture in Southeast Asia include A. H. Christie, "The Megalithic Problem in Southeast Asia," and I. C. Glover, B. Bronson, and D. T. Bayard,

"Comment on 'Megaliths' in South East Asia," both in R. B. Smith and W. Watson (Eds.), *Early South East Asia*. Oxford: Oxford University Press, 1979. For an annotated bibliography, see H. H. E. Loofs, *Elements of the Megalithic Culture in South East Asia*, Canberra: Australian National University Press, 1976.

24. See note 20.

25. For discussion of early Indic sculptural traditions in Bali and the cult of kings, see W. F. Stutterheim, *Indian Influences on Old Balinese Art*. London: The India Society, 1935, *passim*. Clay seals and other objects are on display at the archaeological museum in Pejeng. The inscriptions on seals discovered by 1953 are described in Roelef Goris, *Prasasti Bali* (2 Vols.). Lembaga Bahasa dan Budaya, Universitet Indonesia: N. V. Masa Baru, Bandung, 1954, *passim*. The principal references for the Balinese royal inscriptions are: Roelef Goris, *Prasasti Bali I* and *Prasasti Bali II*, Lembaga Bahasa dan Budaya, Universitet Indonesia: N. V. Masa Baru, Bandung, 1954; P. V. van Stein Callenfels, *Epigraphika Balica I*, Verhandelingen van het Koninklijk Bataviaasch Gennootschap van Kunsten en Wetenschappen LXVI, 1926; and more recently, M. M. Sukarto K. Almodjo's publications such as "Prasasti Campagna," *Seri Prasasti No. 1*, Lembaga Purbakala, Gianyar, Bali, 1974; "The Charter of Kapal," B. K. I. deel 130, 1973, etc. For a list of Javanese inscriptions to 1952, see L. C. Damais, "Etudes d'Epigraphie Indonesienne III: Liste des Principales Inscriptions Datees de l'Indonesie", *BEFEO* 46, pp. 1–105.

26. Goris, Vol. I (1954) (*op. cit.*), pp. 53–54.

27. Dr. M. M. Sukarto K. Atmodjo has collected much interesting information about the reign of Anak Wungcu in "Struktur Pemerintahan dan Masjarakat Djaman Anak Wungcu" (The Structure of Government and Society in the Reign of Anak Wungcu), based on the 28 inscriptions dating from his reign (±1049–1077 A.D.). This article was published in a limited edition by the Panitia Penjusun Buku Standard/Sejarah Sasional Indonesia, Bali, 1972. See also Stutterheim (1935), and Goris (1953). For a general exposition (albeit relating to Javanese dynasties of a later date), see Soemarsaid Moertono, *State and Statecraft in Old Java: A Study of the Later Mataram Period, 16th to 19th Century*. Ithaca: Cornell Modern Indonesia Project Monograph Series No. 43, 1968.

On early Balinese inscriptions, see the references in note 25 (above). On taxation and royal administration in Java, see Jan Wisseman, "Markets and Trade in Pre-Islamic Java," presented at the Conference on Trade in Ancient Southeast Asia: The Role of Economic Exchange in Cultural and Social Development. Ann Arbor, Michigan, March 22–24, 1976. Published in K. Hutterer (Ed.), *Economic Exchange and Social Interaction in SE Asia*. Ann Arbor: Michigan Papers on SE Asia #11, pp. 197–212.

28. The inscription is Sembiran All, Goris, p. 209, dating 975 A.D., from Roelef Goris, *Prasasti Bali I*, Lembaga Bahasa dan Budaya, Universitet Indonesia: N. V. Masa Baru, Bandung, 1954, p. 17.

29. Goris (1954), *op. cit.*

30. M. M. Sukarto K. Atmodjo, "Preliminary Report on the Copper-Plate Inscription of Asahduren," *B. K. I.* 126, 1970, pp. 221–222.

31. *Ibid.*

32. The terms *"kulagotra"* and *"mahagotra"* are still used as elevated, High Balinese words for large descent groups (commonly called *soroh*). The magazine *Warta Dutta Warga*, for example, an organ of the Pasek *sorohs*, refers to both *mahagotra* and *kulagotra*: see *Warta Dutta Warga*, Mei, 1975 (No. 15) *passim*.

33. Goris (1954), *op. cit.* Bebetin Al, Goris, 002, 26, pp. 4–5, 896 A.D.

34. P. J. van Stein Callenfels, 1926, pp. 14–18, *op. cit.*

35. Kautilya, *Arthasastra* in William H. McNeill and Jean W. Sedlar (Eds.), *Classical India*. New York: Oxford University Press, 1969, p. 25.

36. See the discussion of Sanskrit influence on Old Javanese in P. J. Zoetmulder,

Kalangwan, *A Survey of Old Javanese Literature*. The Hague: Martinus Nijhoff, 1974, pp. 8–12.

37. *Ibid.*, pp. 251–256.
38. *Ibid.*, pp. 275–276.
39. *Ibid.*, p. 163.
40. *Ibid.*, p. 276.
41. On this see Zoetmulder, *op. cit.*, pp. 165–173.
42. Goris (1954), *op. cit.* I am indebted to Jan Wisseman for this English translation.
43. Quoted in Miguel Covarrubias *Island of Bali*. New York: Alfred Knopf, 1937, pp. 377–383.
44. John Crawfurd, *A History of the Indian Archipelago*, Vol. II (3 vols.). Edinburgh and London: A. Constable, 1820, p. 257.
45. Clifford Geertz (1980), p. 13.
46. See Paul Wheatley (1971), p. 259.
47. Clifford Geertz (1980), p. 42–43.
48. *Ibid.*, p. 124.
49. Marshall Sahlins, "Poor Man, Rich Man, Big Man, Chief: Political Types in Melanesia and Polynesia," *Comparative Studies in Society and History*, Vol. 5, No. 3, 1963, p. 300.
50. Paul Kirchhoff, "The Principle of Clanship in Human Society," in Morton Fried (Ed.), *Readings in Anthropology Vol. II*. New York: Thomas Y. Crowell, 1964, p. 268.
51. *Ibid.*, p. 267.
52. Geertz (1980), p. 30.
53. Geertz (1980), p. 27. In addition to these endogamous marriages, princes also attempted to ally themselves with other powerful descent groups, often of lower "caste" (Varna) status. These hypergamous marriages were known as *wargi*. Ideally, the eldest son of such a union would be established in a "palace" in his mother's territory, thus helping to bind his mother's descent group to his father's court. A great many tiny "courts" were established in the countryside in this way. Thus, each cadet line could generate its own cadet lines, while also attempting to bind itself to the core line through patriparallel marriage. For alternative views of marriage and court structure, see Geertz (1980) and Boon (1977).
54. Geertz (1980), p. 16.
55. Willard Hanna, *Bali Profile*, (1976), p. 70.
56. Hanna (1976), p. 33.
57. Hanna (1976), pp. 41–42. For a Balinese view of the war against the northern princedom of Buleleng, see P. J. Worseley, *Babad Buleleng: A Balinese Dynastic Genealogy*. The Hague, 1972.
58. Hanna (1976), pp. 42–43. The remainder of this account is based on Hanna (1976), pp. 46–49, 60–75.

CHAPTER 3

1. Personal communication.
2. Sumanasantaka 28.26., quoted in Zoetmulder (1974), pp. 171, 535.
3. The variety of Balinese temples, and the relationship of institutional systems to temples, has been repeatedly noted by ethnographers. Thus, Goris began an article on the temple of Besakih with the following general remarks about the significance of temples:

As a prefatory remark it may be repeated, though no doubt unnecessarily, that Bali is "the land of a thousand temples." Every village community maintains at least three, and usually more. There is a temple for every sawah complex and for every dam. On every large mountain there is a temple, and in the village temples there are altars and shrines dedicated to these high peaks. Each family has its own temple, and every large genealogical group has its own particular sanctuary. The estimate of a thousand is unduly modest.

During the heavy earthquake in 1917 there were, according to official statistics, no less than 2,431 temples destroyed. The affected region was only about one-ninth of the total area of the island, and the locality around Lake Batur, where the tremors were particularly severe, is the least densely populated. So it would be no exaggeration to assess the number of temples in all Bali at rather more than twenty thousand.

R. Goris, Pura Besakih Through the Centuries, in J. L. Swellengrebel (Ed.), *Bali: Further Studies in Life, Thought and Ritual.* The Hague: W. Van Hoeve, Ltd., 1969, p. 91.

4. See Kawaguchi and Kyuma, *Paddy Soils in Tropical Asia,* Monograph #10 of the Center for Southeast Asian Studies, Kyoto University, English version, University Press of Hawaii, Honolulu, 1977, Chapt. 3, "General Features of Paddy Soils in Tropical Asia," esp. p. 57.

5. Kawaguchi and Kyuna (above) estimate nitrogen fixation in the surface water of a paddy field, "which is probably mostly carried out by blue green algae," at 3.2 kg N/ha in the presence of rice plants and 10.9 kg N/ha in their absence (p. 61). They note: "Since other natural sources of nitrogen, such as rainfall and irrigation water, are hardly likely to account for the amount of nitrogen used by the rice crop, it is obvious that microbial nitrogen fixation made it possible to produce more than one ton of paddy per hectare continuously over hundreds of years under conditions where no methods of replenishing fertility have been adopted" (p. 60).

6. *Ibid.,* p. 39.

7. *Ibid.,* pp. 39–47.

8. Clifford Geertz (1980), p. 80.

9. F. A. Liefrinck, "Rice Culturation in Northern Bali" (1887), reprinted in J. L. Swellengrebel et al., *Bali: Life, Thought and Ritual.* W. van Hoeve: The Hague and Bandung, 1960, pp. 34–37.

10. Statistical data were collected by the author from each district (Kecamaton) or region (Kabupaten) during 1975–1976 and pertain to the year 1975.

11. Hildred and Clifford Geertz (1975), p. 76.

12. For lucid presentations of the uses of stochastic (nondeterministic) models in evaluating nonexperimental data, see Hubert M. Blalock, Jr., *Causal Inferences in Non-experimental Research.* Chapel Hill: The University of North Carolina Press, 1964 (see especially Chap. 3); and D. J. Bartholomew, *Stochastic Models for Social Processes,* 2nd Ed. New York and London: John Wiley and Sons, 1973 (on Markov chains, see Chapter 2).

CHAPTER 4

1. Paul Ricoeur, "What is a Text? Explanation and Interpretation", in David Rasmussen (Ed.), *Mythic-Symbolic Language and Philosophical Anthropology: A Constructive Interpretation of the Thought of Paul Ricoeur,* The Hague: Nijhoff, 1971, p. 138.

2. "Interview with Edward Said", *Diacritics,* Vol. 6, No. 3, 1976, p. 41. For Said's critique of Ricouer, see Edward Said, "The Text, the World, the Critic", in Josue Harari (Ed.), *Textual Strategies: Perspectives in Post-Structuralist Criticism,* Ithaca: Cornell University Press, 1979, pp. 164–166.

3. Mattani Rutnin, "Transformations of Thai Concepts of Aesthetics," paper presented to the Second S.S.R.C. Conference on Southeast Asian Aesthetics, Cornell University, August 24–26, 1980, unpublished.

4. Shelly Errington, "Some Comments on Style in the Meanings of the Past," *Journal of Asian Studies*, Vol. XXXVIII, No. 2, February 1979, pp. 231–244.

5. P. J. Zoetmulder, Kalangwan, *A Survey of Old Javanese Literature*, The Hague: Nijhoff, 1974, p. 175.

6. *Ibid.*, p. 173.

7. *Ibid.*, pp. 209–210.

8. Diane Wolkstein, "Master of the Shadow Play", *Parabola*, Vol. IV, No. 4, 1979, p. 27.

9. *Ibid.*

10. Zoetmulder, *op. cit.*, p. 209.

11. Alton Becker, "Text-Building, Epistemiology and Aesthetics in Javanese Shadow Theater," in Becker and Yengoyan (1979).

12. John Emigh, "Playing with the Past," *The Drama Review*, Vol. 23, No. 2, 1979, pp. 11–49.

13. *Ibid.*

14. C. C. Berg's analysis of language in Old Javanese poetry is contained in his "Javaansche geschiedschriving," in *Geschiedenis van Nederlandsch-Indie*, onder leiding van F. W. Stapel, K.N.I.: Amsterdam, 1938, II, pp. 5–148.

15. Zoetmulder, *op. cit.*, p. 167.

16. Michel Foucault, *The Order of Things* (Les Mots et Les Choses), London: Tavistock; New York: Pantheon, 1970, p. 36.

17. Judith Becker, "Time and Tune in Java," in A. Becker and A. Yengoyan (Eds.), *The Imagination of Reality: Essays in Southeast Asian Coherence Systems*. Norwood, New Jersey: Ablex, 1979.

18. Geertz's discussion of Balinese theories of time occurs in *The Interpretation of Cultures*. New York: Basic Books, 1973, pp. 391–98.

19. Harry J. Jerison, "Paleoneurology and the Evolution of Mind," *Scientific American*, Vol. 234, No. 1, January 1976, p. 101. See also H. J. Jerison, *Evolution of the Brain and Intelligence*. Academic Press, 1973; Philip V. Tobias, *The Brain in Hominid Evolution*. New York: Columbia University Press, 1971.

CHAPTER 5

1. Sherry B. Ortner, *Sherpas Through Their Rituals*. Cambridge: Cambridge University Press, 1978, p. 6.

2. Clifford Geertz, *The Interpretation of Cultures*. New York: Basic Books, Inc., 1973, p. 183.

3. Victor Turner, *Dramas, Fields and Metaphors*. Ithaca, New York: The Cornell University Press, 1974, p. 14.

4. Beryl de Zoete and Walter Spies, *Dance and Drama in Bali*. London: Faber and Faber, 1938, 116–134.

5. Jane Belo, *Bali: Rangda and Barong*, American Ethnological Society Monographs, No. 16, 1949.

6. Margaret Mead and Gregory Bateson, *Balinese Character*. New York: Special Publications of the New York Academy of Sciences, Vol. II, 1942, *passim*.

7. James A. Boon *The Anthropological Romance of Bali*, New York: Cambridge University Press, 1977, p. 103.

CHAPTER 6

1. See B. J. Haga, "Bali Aga", *Adatrechtbundel XXIII: Java en Bali* The Hague: Martinus Nijhoff, 1924: 453–469; V. E. Korn, *Het Adatrecht van Bali*, The Hague: G. Naeff, 1932, pp. 75–100 and *passim.*; Noord-Balishe desa monographieen, *Adatrechtbundel XXXVII*, 1934, pp. 1–347; C. J. Grader, "Dorpsbestuur en Tempelbeheer op Noesa Penida", *DJAWA* 17 Nos. 5 and 6, pp. 372–391, etc.

2. Not all villages known as "Bali Aga" are remote, however, nor (as will be shown) are they identical in their customs. The village of Tenganan Pagringsingan is the only Bali Aga village which has been the subject of an entire monograph (for that matter, it is the only village anywhere in Bali to which an entire monograph has been devoted). But Tenganan lies in the midst of fertile *sawah* fields well within the effective borders of the former *negara* of Karangasem. How could such a village be "Bali Aga"?

According to V. E. Korn, author of the monograph on Tenganan, the village achieved a partial autonomy not by physical remoteness or poverty, but by virtue of its extreme wealth, which enabled it to develop a special relationship to the courts.

> It is clear from various stipulations in the *desa* constitution (which, as was seen above, is a record of what could be remembered of the old charter destroyed by fire) that the ruler who drafted the original charter had the aim of making Tenganan a *perdikan desa* (a village freed from certain taxes and obligations). When I enquired of Anak Agung Agung Bagus Jelantik, the head of the former ruling family of Karangasem, why Tenganan enjoyed such a large degree of autonomy, and why after the fire the people of the village went to Klungkung (capital of the Dewa Agung, theoretically the supreme ruler of Bali) rather than Singaradja, capital of the rulers of Karangasem, who are nominally subjects of Klungkung, he was unable to give me an explanation: Tenganan had been left to its own devices even in early times .... According to Tengananese tradition, the ruler of Bedahulu made Tenganan a *perdikan desa* and granted it charter. Now the successor to Bedahulu is the Dewa Agung of Klungkung, and the ruler of Karangasem is his viceroy; hence the Tengananese consider only what the Dewa Agung has ordained to be valid for their *desa*, and the boundaries of the various principalities have little significance for them: above the village level they recognize only the whole of Bali. (page 362)

This luxurious independence had its basis, according to Korn, in the large annual "gift" presented by the village to the court at Karangasem.

> In earlier times the *desa* of Tenganan was even more independent of the royal administration than it is today. No services were rendered and no taxes were paid, either in money or in kind. Each year the *desa* presented the ruler a tributary gift in lieu of meeting royal rights such as the claim to property of people dying without children, the usual fees on weddings and land taxes, and each year a fifth of that gift was returned to the *desa* as a sign that the relationship between the ruler and the village was to continue in the same way. (page 363)

Actually, at the time of Korn's study (1926), informants remembered that men of Tenganan had participated in a military expedition by the court of Karangasem against Mengwi, in the late 19th century, and the village had other miscellaneous duties imposed by the court, such as helping with the upkeep of a temple. Korn's monograph, and his extensive papers on Tenganan and Karangasem (housed in the library of the Koninklijk Instituut voor Taal, Land en Volkenkunde in Leiden) demonstrate that the village was richly endowed with rice fields and that it used its wealth to maintain a special relationship with the courts in order to preserve its autonomy so far as possible. Korn studied the village only 18 years after the Dutch conquest, so that the precolonial relationships between Tenganan and the courts were living memories.

From the standpoint of my thesis on the role of the arts in village change, it is interesting that, as Korn observed,

> Music, dance and drama are little developed in Tenganan. . . . Consequently, when in earlier times the rulers of Karangasem passed the night in the village, they had to provide their own dancing girls and boys, for the *desa* could not supply them. The *desa* does not own a *wayang* set, nor is the *wayang* performed there. (page 313)

In fact certain of the arts flourish in Tenganan—the village owns an ancient *gamelan selonding*, and boys and girls belong to dance clubs—but the arts of Tenganan are by and large in the Bali Aga pattern. (Quotations are from the English translation of Korn's *De Dorpsrepubliek Tenganan PaGringsingan* in *Bali: Studies in Life, Thought, Ritual*. The Hague: W. van Hoeve, 1960.)

3. F. A. Liefrinck, "Grondenrecht van Desa Djoelah", *Adatrechtbundel*, Vol. 37, pp. 346–347 (my translation).

4. Jap Kunst, *Hindu-Javanese Musical Instruments*. The Hague: Martinus Nijhoff, 1968, pp. 75–81.

5. De Zoete and Spies (1939), *op. cit.*, p. 56.

6. Claire Holt, "The Baris Jangkang", *Djawa* (1937), p. 135.

7. De Zoete and Spies, *op. cit.*, p. 55.

CHAPTER 7

1. R. Goris, "Een plechtige bede in een Eeeuwenoud Heiligdom", *Indonesie*, 2, pp. 11–18, 1949; "De poera Besakih, Bali's rijkstempel", *DJAWA*, 17, pp. 261–280, 1937.

2. R. Goris, "The State Temple of Besakih", in J. L. Swellengrebel (Ed.), *Bali: Further Studies in Life, Thought, Ritual*. The Hague: W. van Hoeve, 1960, p. 237.

3. Ibid., p. 235.

4. Willard Hanna, *Bali Profile*, (AUFS). Lebanon, N.H.: Whitman Press, 1976, 114–115.

5. Speech by I Gusti Kaler.

CONCLUSION

1. W. F. Stutterheim, *Indian Influences on Old-Balinese Art*. London: The India Society, 1935, p. 7.

Bibliography

Adatrechtbundels: I (1910); X (1915); XV (1918); XVIII (1919); XXII (1923); XXIII (1924); XXIX (1928); XXXIII (1930); XXXVII (1934); XXXIX (1937), The Hague.

Ardana, I Gusti Gdi, "Pengertian Pura di Bali", Proyek Pemiliharaan dan Pengembangan Kebudayaan Daerah Bali, Denpasar, 1971.

Artaud, A. *The Theater and Its Double*, English translation by M. C. Richards. New York: Grove Press, 1958.

Bagus, Dr. Gusti Ngurah. "Sistem Pola Menetap Masyarakat Bali", Fakultas Sastra, Udayana University, Denpasar, 1969.

_____, "Pertentangan kasta dalam bentuk baru pada Masyarakat Bali", *UNUD*, Denpasar, 1969.

_____, "Clan dalam Hubungannya dengan pola menetap di desa Sembiran", *UNUD*, Denpasar, 1968.

_____, "Tjatatan Singkat mengenai Dialect Sembiran dan Spang di Bali", Lembaga Bahasa Nasional, Singaradja, 1971.

_____, "Surya Kanta: Modern Kewangsaan movement of the Jaba caste in Bali", *Masyarakat Indonesia*, No. 2, 1975, pp. 153–163.

_____ (Ed.), *Masalah Bahasa Bali*, UNUD, Denpasar, 1975.

_____ (Ed.), *Bali Dalam Sentuhan Pariwisata*, UNUD, Denpasar, 1975.

Bandem, I Made, *Serba Neka Wayang Kulit Bali*, Denpasar, 1975.

Bateson, Gregory, and Mead, Margaret, *Balinese Character*. New York: Special Publications of the New York Academy of Sciences, Vol. II, 1942 (reissued 1962).

Becker, Alton, "Notes on the Ramayana in Modern Java," Association for Asian Studies, Toronto, 1973 (unpublished).

Becker, A., and Yengoyan, A. (Eds.), *The Imagination of Reality*. Norwood, N.J.: Ablex Publishing Co., 1979.

Belo, Jane, (Ed.), *Traditional Balinese Culture*. New York: Columbia University Press, 1970.

———, *Bali: Temple Festival*. Monographs of the American Ethnological Society, XXII, New York, 1953.

———, *Bali: Rangda and Barong*. New York: American Ethnological Society Monograph, 16. J. J. Augustin: 1949.

Berg, C. C. (Ed.), *Kidung Pamañcangah, de geschiedenis van het rijk van Gelgel*. Javaansch-Balische historische geschriften, I. Santpoort, 1929.

———, *De Middeljavaansche historische traditie*, Dissertation, University of Leiden, Santpoort, 1927.

———, *Babad Bla-Batuh*. Santpoort, 1932.

Bloemen Waanders, F. L. van, "Aanteckening omtrent de zeden en gebruiken der Balinezen, inzonder-heit die van Boeleleng", *T.B.G.*, Dl. VIII, 3e Serie, Dl. II, 1859, pp. 105–279.

———, "Bijdragen tot de kennis van het Eiland Bali", *T.N.I.*, Dl. VIII, 13e Serie, Dl. II, 1859, pp. 105–279.

Booms, P. G., "Precis des Expeditions de l'Armée Neerlandaise des Indes Orientales contre les Princes de Bali de 1846–1849," Breda, 1850.

Boon, J. "Dynastic Dynamics: Caste and Kinship in Bali Now". Ph.D. dissertation, Department of Anthropology, University of Chicago, 1973.

———, *The Anthropological Romance of Bali, 1597–1972*. Cambridge and New York: Cambridge University Press, 1977.

Bosch, F. D. K. "Notes archeologiques," *BEFEO*, XXXI, 1931, pp. 485–497.

———, "C. C. Berg and Ancient Javanese History," *B.K.I.* deel 112, pp. 1–24.

Brandes, J. L. A., *Beschrijving der Javaansche, Balineesche en Sasaksche handschriften aangetroffen in de nalatenschap van H. N. van der Tuuk*. 4 vols. Batavia: Boccard, 1901–1926.

———, "De koperen platen van Sembiran". *T.B.G.*, XXXIII, pp. 16–56, 1890.

Brandon, James R., *Theater in Southeast Asia*, Cambridge: Harvard University Press, 1967.

Coedes, Georges, *The Indianized States of Southeast Asia*, translated by S. B. Cowing. Honolulu: East-West Center Press, 1968 (French edition, Paris: Editions E. de Boccard, 1964).

Cool, W., *De Lombok Expeditie*. 's Grauenhage, 1896.

Covarrubias, Miguel, *Island of Bali*. New York: Alfred Knopf, 1936.

Crucq, K. C., *Bijdrage tot de kennis van het Balisch doodenritueel*. Dissertation, University of Leiden, Santpoort, 1928.

Damais, L. C., "Études Balinaises". Paris: *BEFEO*, XLIV, pp. 121–140, 1947–1950.

Damsté, H. T., "Balische Oudheden," Oudheidkundig Verslag uitgegeven door het Bataviaasch Genootschap van kunsten en Wetenschappen, 1922.

De Zoete, Beryl, and Walter Spies, *Dance and Drama in Bali*. London: Faber and Faber, 1938.

Departemen Pekerjaan Umum dan Tenaga Listrik, "Laporan study mengenai lingkungan banjar di Bali," Dir. Djen. Cipta Karya, Dep. P. U., Bali, 1972.

Djawa, Tijdschrift van Java-Instituut, 1936–1937.

Eck, R. van, "Schetsen van het Eiland Bali", *T.N.I.* Nieuwe Serie, VII–IX, pp. 1878–1880.

Foucault, Michel, *The Order of Things.* New York: Random House, 1973 (French Edition, Paris: Editions Gallimard, 1966).

Friederich, R., *The Civilization and Culture of Bali.* Calcutta: Susil Gupta (India) Private Ltd., 1959.

Geertz, Clifford, "Form and variation in Balinese village structure," *American Anthropologist,* 1957, 61, pp. 991–1012.

————, "Tihingan: A Balinese Village," in R. M. Koentjaraningrat (Ed.), *Villages in Indonesia,* Ithaca, New York: Cornell University Press, 1967.

————, *The Interpretation of Cultures.* New York: Basic Books, 1973.

————, *Negara: The Theater State in Nineteenth Century Bali,* Princeton, New Jersey: Princeton University Press, 1980.

————, "Teknonymy in Bali: Parenthood, age grading and genealogical amnesia," *Journal of the Royal Anthropological Institute,* 94, 1964.

————, and Hildred Geertz, *Kinship in Bali.* Chicago: The University of Chicago Press, 1975.

Geertz, Hildred, "The Balinese Village," in G. W. Skinner (Ed.), *Local, National and Regional Loyalties in Indonesia.* New Haven: Yale University Southeast Asian Studies, 1959.

Gorer, Geoffrey, *Bali and Angkor, or Looking at Life and Death.* Boston: Little, Brown and Co., 1936.

Goris, R., *Bijdrage tot de Kennis der Oud-Javaansche en Balinesche Theologie,* Ph.D. thesis Leiden, Vros, Leiden, 1926.

————, Het Geloof der Balineezen, *DJAWA,* 8, pp. 41–49, 1928.

————, "De positie der Pandé Wesi," *MK,* 1/2, pp. 41–52, 1929; English translation, 1960.

————, "Overeenkomst tusschen de Javaansche en Balische feestkalender, *DJAWA,* 12, pp. 110–113, 1932.

————, "Bali's hoogtijden," *TBG,* 73, pp. 436–452, 1933; English translation, 1960.

————, "Het Godsdienstig karakter der Balische dorpsgemeenschap," *DJAWA,* 15, pp. 1–16, 1935; English translation, 1960.

————, "Overzicht van de Belangrijkste literatuur betreffende de cultuur van Bali 1920–1935," *MK,* 5, pp. 15–44, 1937.

————, "De poera Běsakih, Bali's rijkstempel," *DJAWA,* 17, pp. 261–280, 1937.

————, "Bali's tempelwezen," *DJAWA,* 18, pp. 30–42, 1938; English translation, 1960.

————, "Een merkwaardige plechtigheid in een Bijzonder heiligdom," in collaboration with Prof. G. H. Bousquet, *DJAWA,* 19, pp. 46–53, 1939.

————, "Het groote Tienjaarlijksche feest te Sělat," *DJAWA,* 19, pp. 94–112, 1939.

————, "Een ouderwetsche plechtigheid te Koekoeb," *DJAWA,* 19, pp. 142–145, 1939.

_____, "Een plechtige bede in een Eeuwenoud Heiligdom," *Indonesië*, 2, pp. 11–18, 1949.

_____, and Dr. P. L. Dronkers, *Bali, Cults and Customs*. Published by the Government of the Republic of Indonesia, 1953.

Grader, C. J., "Twee-deeling in het Oud-Balische Dorp.," *MK*, 5, pp. 45–72, 1937.

_____, "Madènan (désa-monographie)," *MK*, 5, pp. 73–122, 1937.

_____, "Dorpsbestuur en tempelbeheer op Noesa Pěnida," *DJAWA*, 17, pp. 372–391, 1937.

_____, "De poera Pěmajoen van Bandjar Tegal," *DJAWA*, 19, pp. 330–367, 1939; English translation in Bali, 1960.

_____, "Poera madoewé Karang, Noord-Balisch agrarisch Heiligdom," *MK*, 12, pp. 1–37, 1940.

_____, "De rijkstempels van Měngwi," *TBG*, 83, pp. 394–423, 1949; English translation in Bali, 1960.

Hanna, Willard, *Bali Profile*, (AUFS). Lebanon, New Hampshire: Whitman Press, 1976.

Helbig, K., "Noesa penida, het 'Bandieten-eiland'," *TN*, XI, pp. 329–348, 1939.

Holt, Claire, *Art in Indonesia: Continuities and Change*. Ithaca, New York: Cornell University Press, 1967.

Hooykaas, Christiaan, "The Balinese Sengguhu-priest," in John Bastin and R. Roolvink (Eds.), *Malayan and Indonesian Studies*. Oxford University Press, 1974.

_____, *Agama Tirtha*. Amsterdam: Verhandelingen KAW, Afd. L, Nieuwe Reeks, Deel 70/4, 1964.

_____, *Surya-Sevana, the Way to God of a Balinese Siva Priest*. Amsterdam: Verhandelingen KAW, Afd. L., Nienwe Reeks, Deel 72/3, 1966.

Hooykaas, C., and T. Gondriaan, *Stuti and Stava*. Amsterdam: Verhandelingen KAW, Nienwe Reeks, Deel 76, 1971.

Hunger, F. W. T., "Eenige aanteenkeningen over Noor-Balische Bali Aga Desa's Sidatapa en Pedawa", *DJAWA*, 17, pp. 367–371, 1937.

Kant, I., *Kritik der reinen Vernunft, Transzendentale Aestetik #1*, E. Cassirer, III (ed.), Berlin, 1923.

Kat Angelino, P. de., "Over de smeden en eenige andere ambachtslieden op Bali," *TBG*, LX, pp. 207–265, 1921, LXI, pp. 370–424, 1922.

_____, "De léak op Bali," *TBG*, LX pp. 1–44, 1921.

Kawaguchi and Kyuma, *Paddy Soils in Tropical Asia*. Monograph No. 10 of the Kyoto University Center for Southeast Asian Studies. English version, Honolulu: The University Press of Hawaii, 1977.

Korn, Victor Emmanuel, *Het Adatrecht van Bali*. 2nd Ed., The Hague, 1932.

_____, "Noesa penida," *Cultureel Indie*, VI, pp. 97–109, 1944.

_____, *De Dorpsrepubliek Tnganan Pagringsingan*. Santpoort: K.N.I., 1933.

Kristeller, Paul O., "The Modern System of the Arts" in *Renaissance Thought II*. Princeton: Princeton University Press, 1965.

Krom, N. J., *Hindoe-Javaansche Geschiedenis*, 2nd ed. The Hague, 1931.

Kunst, J., *Hindu-Javanese Musical Instruments*. The Hague: Martinus Nijhoff, 1968.

Landsberg, Marge E., "The icon in semiotic theory," *Current Anthropology*, Vol. 21, No. 1, pp. 93–95, Feb., 1980.

Lansing, J. Stephen, *Evil in the Morning of the World*. Ann Arbor: Michigan Papers on South and Southeast Asia No. 6, 1974.

Lekkerkerker, C., "Bali 1800–1814," BKI, LXXXII, pp. 315–388, 1926.

————, "De kastenmaatschappij in Britsch-Indië en op Bali," *MM*, II, pp. 175–213, 300–334.

————, "*Bali en Lombok: Overzicht der litteratuur omtrent deze Eilanden tot Einde 1919*," Rijswijk: VIG, 1920.

Liefrinck, F. A., *Bali en Lombok: Geschriften*. Amsterdam: BKI, 1927.

————, "*Grondenrecht van desa Djoelah*," Adatrechtbundel 37, The Hague: Martinus Nijhoff, 1934, pp. 346–347.

————, "De residentie Bali en Lombok na het jaar 1894," *V.I.G.*, pp. 137–166, 1902.

Lingensz, Hernout, "Bali 1597", *B.K.I.*, 2 de r., Dl. I (Dl. V), pp. 203–234, 1856.

Maquet, J., *Introduction to Aesthetic Anthropology*. McCaleb Module in Anthropology. New York: Addison Wesley, 1971.

Medhurst, W. H., "Short Account of the Island of Bali, Particularly of Bali Bailing," in J. H. Moor, *Notices of the Indian Archipelago and Adjacent Countries*. Singapore, 1837.

Mershon, Katharane E., *Seven Plus Seven*. New York: Vantage Press, 1971.

Nieuwenkamp, W. O. J., *Bali en Lombok*, 3 vols. Amsterdam: Edam, 1906–1910.

Pierce, Charles S., *Collected Papers*. Cambridge: Harvard University Press, 1931.

Pigeand, T., *Java in the Fourteenth Century*. 5 vols. The Hague: Koninklijk Instituut, Martinus Nijhoff, 1966.

Raka, I Gusti Gde., *Monografi pulau Bali*. Djakarta: Pusat Djawatan Pertanian Rakjat, 1955.

Rutnin, Mattani Mpjdara, "Transformation of the Thai concepts of aesthetics," Conference on Southeast Asian Aesthetics, Cornell University, August 23–26, 1978 (unpublished).

Sanggra, Made, *Babad Sukawati*. Indonesian edition, private printing, Denpasar, 1975.

Slametmuljana, *A Story of Majapahit*. Singapore: Singapore University Press, 1976.

Spies, Walter, and Beryl De Zoete, *Dance and Drama in Bali*, New York: Harper's, 1939.

Spies, Walter, "Das grosse fest in Dorfe Trunjan (Insel Bali)," *TNI*, LXXIII, pp. 220–256, 1933.

Stutterheim, W. F., *Indian Influences on Old-Balinese Art*. London: The India Society, 1935.

Sugriwa, I. G. B., *Hari Raya Bali Hindu*, Denpasar: Balimas, 1952.

————, Babad Pasĕk, ditĕrdjĕmahkan kĕdalam bahasa Indonesia dari babonnja jang bĕrbahasa Bali. Denpasar: Balimas, 1957.

Trinkaus, C., *In Our Image and Likeness: Humanity and Divinity in Italian Humanist Thought*, Vol. II. Chicago: Univ. of Chicago Press, 1970.

Turner, Victor, *Dramas, Fields and Metaphors*. Ithaca, New York: Cornell University Press, 1974.

Wescott, Roger W., "Linguistic Iconism," *Language*, 47, pp. 416–28.

Wolkstein, Diana, "Master of the Shadow Play," *Parabola: Myth and the Quest for Meaning*. New York: Society for the Study of Myth and Tradition, 1980.

Zoetmulder, P. J., *Kalangwan, A Survey of Old Javanese Literature*. The Hague: Martinus Nijhoff, 1974.

Index

Acton, Lord John, 30
Adatrecht (Korn), 114
"Aesthetic Anthropology" (Maquet), 9
aesthetics, 9–10; Thai, 77
Africa, art in, 9
Agasthya, 33
agriculture, rice production (*see* rice production)
Anak Wungcu, 27
Angkorean kingdom, 145
Angkor temple, 21
animism, 76
anniversary festivals, 61–65
Aquinas, St. Thomas, 8
archaeology, 16, 17, 24–31, 147
architecture, 72; Hindu/Buddist, 17
aristocracy, 39–41
"Arjuna Wijaya" (poem), 82
art: concepts of, 8–10, 76; culture and, 10–12; religious, 10, 11; ritual compared with, 93, 94, 96, 97, 111
Artaud, Antonin, 2
Arthasāstra, 32
artists, 29–30
Ashanti tribe, 9
Astika, 87
Atharva-Veda, 19

Badung, 134; massacre of, 46–47
Bakhen, 20–21
Bālaputradēva (Maharaja), 17
Balavavarman, 17
Bali: civilization, sources of, 3; conquest by Dutch, 5, 6; physical description, 3

Bali Aga, 13, 113–127, 147; temples, 114, 115–117
Bali Mula, 113
Balinese language, 83, 87
Bangli, 134
Baumgarten, Alexander, 9, 10
bebali performances, 95–97
Bebetin, 30
Becker, Alton, 52, 83
Becker, Judith, 89
Beginnings: Intention and Method, 75
Belo, Jane, 2, 96, 97
Berg, C.C., 86
Besakih (shrine), 25, 130, 131, 132, 133
Bhāratayuddha, 33
Bhatara Turun Kabeh, 134
Bhojadeva, 19
Buana Agung, (Great Realm), 81, 82, 139, 140
Buana Alit (Small Realm), 139, 140
Boas, Franz, 11, 12, 15
Boon, James, 104, 107
Borobudur, 17
Brahma, 21, 98
Brahmana caste, 27, 101, 144, 145
Brahmana hypothesis, 15, 16
Buddhism, 17–18, 23; Hindu/Buddhist sects, 32, 143, 144, 145; Mahāyāna, 18–19
Buleleng, 37, 45, 134
burial customs, 24, 25, 34–36, 65, 66, 94, 106, (*see also* cremation)
Burmese rulers, 36
Buta Yadnya (exorcisms), 140

cadet lines, 41
calendars, 19–21, 53–55, 89
Calonarang, 96–97
Cambodia, 17, 19
caste system, 7, 23, 24, 27, 28, 99,
    101–111, 144, 147; subcastes,
    103–110
caste temples, 99, 101–104, 106–107;
    rituals, 106
Chandi Kalasan, 26
child care, 2
Chomsky, Noam, 91
"Chronicle of King Jayakasunu,"
    135–136
cities, cosmological significance of, 65
civilization sources, 3, 6–7
clan organization, conical, 39–41
clowns (parekan), 90
cockfights, 64
competitive display, 3, 4–5
cosmology: Buddhist, 19–20;
    government and, 33–34; Hindu/
    Buddhist, 3–4, 7, 19–20, 26, 29,
    52, 146; temples as symbols of, 65
courtiers (kaula kawisuda), 6
courts, role of, 3–5, 31, 37–41, 51
court temples, 99, 106
craftsmen, 30
Crawford, John, 35
creativity of Balinese, 1–3
cremation, 34–36, 100, 108
Critique of Pure Reason, 9
culture, art and, 10–12

Dahomey, art in, 9
D'Alembert, Jean, 9
dance, 62, 63; Bali Aga, 119, 124–125;
    creese dance, 64; magic and, 97;
    Thai, 76; troupes, 100, 119
Dance and Drama in Bali, 2
death rituals, 100, 124; burial (see
    burial customs); cremation, 34–36,
    100, 108
Death Temple, 97
demons, 7, 96
Derrida, 88
Dĕvapāladĕva, 17–18
Dewa Agung (Great God), 42, 48, 133

de Zoete, Beryl, 96, 124–125
Diderot, Denis, 8
Discours (d'Alembert), 9
Djagaraga, 45
Djoelah, 119
Dongson culture, 24
drama, multiple languages in, 83–86,
    88
Durga, 96, 135, 141
Dutch conquest, 5, 6, 42, 45–48

Eka Dasa Rudra, 13, 129–142, 147;
    1963, 135–137; 1979, 137–141
elders, 28
Emigh, John, 85
Encyclopedie (Diderot), 8, 9
endogamy, 41
epics, 32, 33; Hindu, 2
Errington, Shelly, 77
eulogies, 33
exorcisms, 140

family relationships, 101–103
festivals (odalans), 6–8, 99–101, 114,
    144; anniversary, 61–65;
    assessment for, 72; Bali Aga, 114,
    115, 119; Eka Dasa Rudra,
    129–142; role of, 51–52, 55, 66,
    73; Sukawati, 6
fine arts, concepts of, 8–10
Foucault, Michel, 75, 86, 87–88
Fourier, Jean Baptiste Joseph, 11

gamelan orchestra, 2, 77, 89, 100, 119,
    121, 124
Ganesha, 27, 144
Geertz, Clifford, 3, 4, 6, 35–36, 38, 41,
    42, 60, 68, 94, 114, 121
Gelgel, 42, 48, 109, 133, 134
gerontocracy, 28
Gianyar, 42, 134
good and evil, struggle between, 80
Gorer, Geoffrey, 2
Goris, Roeloef, 99, 113, 133, 134
Great Council Temple, 98
Great Realm (Buana Agung), 81, 82,
    139, 140
Gunung Agung, 133, 137

Gunung Kawi, 27
Gupta dynasty, 17–18
Gwalior, 19

Hall, Ken, 15
Hang, Jabat, 77
Hanna, Willard, 136
"Hariwangsa" (poem), 33, 86
Heine-Geldern, Robert, 20
hermitages, 28, 144
Hikayal Hang Tuah, 77
Himalayas, monasteries in, 17
Hindu/Buddist sects, 143–145
Hinduism, 17–18, 23, 77
Holt, Claire, 124
holy water, 60–61
hospices, 26–27, 30
household shrines, 56

Indic culture, 12, 15–49; hypotheses
    concerning influence, 15–16;
    negara, 16
Indonesian language, 83, 87
Indra, 82
Inner Temple, 98
inscriptions, 25, 26–27, 30, 31, 34, 98,
    101, 143–145, 148
irrigation, 7, 24, 25, 38, 57, 146

Java (Yavabhūmi), 16, 17, 19;
    literature, 78; seals and sculptures
    in, 25
Jayabhaya, 33
Jayavarman VII, 21, 37
Jelantik (Prince), 42, 45, 83
Jelantik Goes to Blambangan, 84–85, 88
Jembrana, 134
Jerison, A.J., 91–92
jewelry, 24
Jullah, 34, 117–119, 124

Kala, 141
Kandyan kingdom, 65, 145
Kant, Immanuel, 9, 10
Kapakisan, Arya, 133
Karangasem, 45, 133
Karya Taur Agung Eka Dasa Rudra,
    130
kaula kawisuda (see courtiers)
Kesiman, 46
Khmer dynasty, 36–37, 65
"Kidung Tantri" (poem), 84, 85
kingship theories, 3–5, 16, 26, 34, 101
kinship system, 101–103, 121–123
Kirchhoff, Paul, 39
Klungkung, 37, 42, 45, 48, 109,
    133–134
Korn, V.E., 113, 114
Kristellar, Paul, 8
Krṣna (Krishna), 33
Ksatriya caste, 27, 101, 144
Ksatriya hypothesis, 15, 16
Kuba tribe, 9
Kunst, Jap, 124

lake temples, 58
land ownership, 117
Lange, Mads, 41
langö concept, 78–79
language: choice of, 83–86;
    development, 91; nature of,
    75–76, 86, 91–92
Lepchas, 3
Lévi-Strauss, Claude, 115
Liefrinck, F.A., 60, 61–64, 119
life stages, rituals for, 94
linguistics, 11
lost wax casting, 24
Lower World, 52, 55, 66, 73

Mabbett, I.W., 15–16
Machiavelli, Niccolo, 32
Mahābhārata, 2, 32, 33, 85
Mahāyāna Buddhism, 18–19, 26
Majapahit, 42, 133
Majumdar, R.C., 16
Malay culture, 77
mantras, 87
Maospahit, 113, 114
Maquet, Jacques, 9–10
marriage, 123–124
masks, 2
maya (illusion), 52, 55, 78, 81
Mead, Margaret, 1, 2–3, 96, 97

megaliths, 24–25
Melayu, Sejara, 77
Mengwi, 134
metallurgy, 24, 25
Middle Javanese language, 83, 87
Middle World, 52, 55, 56, 65–66, 73,
    93; construction of, 65–73
monasteries, 22–23, 27, 31, 42, 144,
    145; Nālandā, 17–19
monks, 144, 145
Mount Agung, 133, 137
Mountain of Poets, 81
mountain temples, 58
Mount Meru, 20, 65
music, 2, 77, 88–89

Nāgarī lettering, 18
Nālandā, 17–19
Negara: The Balinese Theater State in the
    Nineteenth Century, 6
negara concept, 3–4, 16–17
neighborhood temples, 99–101,
    104–106
Netherlands, conquest of Bali by, 5, 6,
    42, 45–48
Nusa Penida, 124–125

offerings to temple, 51
Old Balinese, 26, 143
Old Javanese, 32, 78, 79, 81, 83–84, 86,
    87
orchestras, 2, 77, 89, 100, 119, 121, 124
Origins Temple (Pura Puseh), 98
Ortner, Sherrie, 94

Pacific Area Travel Agents, 136
padmasana (throne shrine), 6
pageants, 6
painters, 2, 72
palaces, 38; architecture of, 6
Pali, 17
Paris Exposition, 2
Pasek Kayu Selem clan, 134
patterns, prevalence of, 1
Pawilangan Indik Puja Ring Pura Besakih
    (Ceremonies of Worship at the Temple
    of Besakih), 141

Pejeng temple, 24
Pemetjutan massacre, 46
perception, culture and, 10–12
performing arts, 13, 30, 80, 144, 145,
    147; number of groups, 66–70,
    71–73 (see also dance; music)
Perrault, 8
poetry, 78; epics, 2, 32, 33
possession by spirits, 76
Prambanan temple complex, 22
Prince, The, 32
Proto-Austronesian culture, 24
puppetry (wayang), 51, 77, 80–83, 97
Puputan (the Finish), 5, 41–48
pura (see temples)
Pura Balai Agung (Great Council
    Temples), 61, 64
Pura Batu Kau, 58
Pura Desa Gde, 123
Pura Ulun Danau, 58, 59

Rama, 132
Rāmāyana, 2, 32, 85, 87, 132
reading clubs, 79–80, 144
reincarnation, 6, 97, 126
religion, art and, 10, 11
rice production, 38, 57–58, 70–71, 146,
    147; festivals, 51–52, 55, 61–65,
    66, 73; irrigation, 7, 24, 25, 38, 57,
    146
Ricoeur, Paul, 75
rites of passage, 106 (see also life stages,
    rituals for)
ritual, 93–94, 96, 111; art compared
    with, 93, 94, 96, 97; life stages
    and, 94, 106
roads, 27, 28
royal troupes, 144
Rudra (see Siwa)
ruler: divinity of, 7; legitimacy of, 3–4
Rotnin, Mattani, 76

Sahlins, Marshall, 12
Said, Edward, 75
Sāilēndra dynasty, 17
Sang Ratu Cri Candra Bhaya Singha
    Warmadeva, 148

Sanskrit culture, 16, 17, 23, 26, 86, 143; literature, 29, 32, 78, 83, 87
Sanur, 46
Sapir, Edward, 91
"Satyantra in Suvarnadvipa," 15
sawah (see rice production)
sculpture, 2, 25, 72
seals, clay, 25
Sembiran, 116, 117, 120–121
shadow plays (see puppetry [wayang])
Shakespeare, William, 90
Sikkim, 3
Singaraja, 45
Singhamamdawa, 26
Siva (see Siwa)
Siwa, 21, 22, 90, 98, 135, 141; Rudra form, 130
slaves (hulun), 27, 144
Small Realm (Buana Alit), 81
social institutions, temples and, 56
social status, Bali Aga villages, 115
sounding of the texts, 13, 76–77, 79–92, 111, 129, 130, 144, 146, 147
speech, 76, (see also language)
Spies, Walter, 96, 124, 125
statecraft, 32
State Temples (see temples)
Steward, Julian, 24
Stocking, George, 11
Stutterheim, W.F., 147–148
subcastes, 103–110 (see also caste system)
Sudarsana, 21
Sudra social class, 101, 144
Suharto, 141
Sukarno, 136–138
Sukawana Al, 26
Sukawati: court, 5–6; temples, 5, 38, 104, 105, 106, 109–111
Sukhawana, 119–120
"Sumanasāntaka," 75, 78, 79
Sumatra, 17
supernatural, belief in, 7–8
Surya cult, 27, 144
suttee, 34–36
Suvarnadvīpa, 17

Tabanan, 48, 134
taboos, 103, 121
Tai rulers, 36
Tantrism, 76
Tawur sacrifices, 139
taxes, 27, 28, 30, 144
television, 138
temple mountains, 65
temple networks, 12, 13, 38
temples, 144, 145, 146; activation, 51; Angkor, 21; Bali Aga, 114, 115–117; Besakih, 130–133; caste, 99, 101–104, 106–111; Chandi Kalasan, 26; congregations, 55; cosmology symbolized by, 65; court, 99, 106; decoration, 1, 2; distribution, 66; festivals (see festivals); layout, 94, 95; neighborhood (banjar), 99–100, 104; offerings, 27, 28, 51; Pejeng, 24; Puru Batu Kau, 58; Pura Ulun Danau, 58, 59; role, 5–8, 51–52, 58, 65–73, 145, 146; Sukawati, 38, taxes for, 72, 144; theater, 7, 51, 146; Three Great Temples, 98, 104; types, 7; village, 93–111; water, 58, 60–65, 70, 73, 99, 104, 106, 146
texts, nature of, 75–76; sounding of, 76–77, 79–92
Thai aesthetics, 76–77
theater, 2; temple, 7, 51, 146
theater state concept, 35–36, 41–49
theocracy, 33
Three Great Temples, 98, 104
Tibet, 17
time, concept of, 52–55, 73; Bali Aga, 115, 125–126
Tirtha Empul, 148
tombs, 22
tourists, 136, 138
Tower of Babel, 86
trade, 24
translations, 90
Turner, Victor, 94
Tutsi art, 9
"Tutur Rogasenggara," 130

Twalen, 90

Udayadityavarman II, 20
Uma, 141
Upper World, 52, 55, 66, 73

van Hoeval, Friederich, 42
Van Leur, J.C., 16
van Wijick (General), 45
Varmadewa dynasty, 34
Varna caste system, 101, 144
Vedas, 19
Viet Nam, Sinicization in, 16
villages, 2, 28, 30, 93, 98, 104; courts,
    monasteries and, 31; taxes, 144
Vishnu (see Wisnu)
volcanoes, 3, 137

Waisya caste, 27, 101, 144
Waisya hypothesis, 15, 16

Waley, Arthur, 2
wali performances, 94–95
Wallace Line, 24
Warmadeva, 21–23
water temples, 7, 60–65, 70–71, 99,
    106, 146, 147
waterworks, 27, 28
wayang (see puppetry)
Wheatley, Paul, 15, 21
Whorf, Benjamin Lee, 91
Wija, 80, 81
Wisnu, 21, 27, 33, 98, 144
witch drama, 96–97
Wolkstein, Diane, 80
work gangs, 100

Yasodharapura, 20–21, 37

Zoetmulder, P.J., 78–79, 86–87
Zollinger, 42

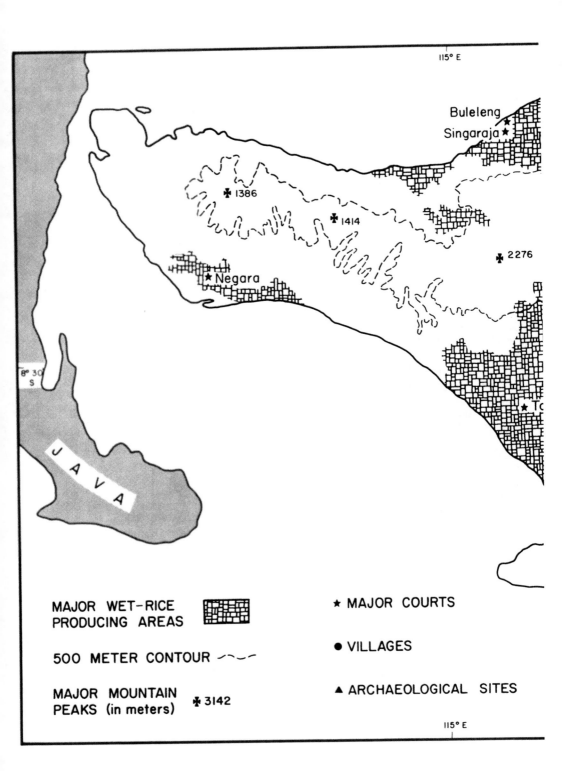

MAJOR WET-RICE
PRODUCING AREAS

500 METER CONTOUR

MAJOR MOUNTAIN
PEAKS (in meters)   ✚ 3142

★ MAJOR COURTS

● VILLAGES

▲ ARCHAEOLOGICAL SITES

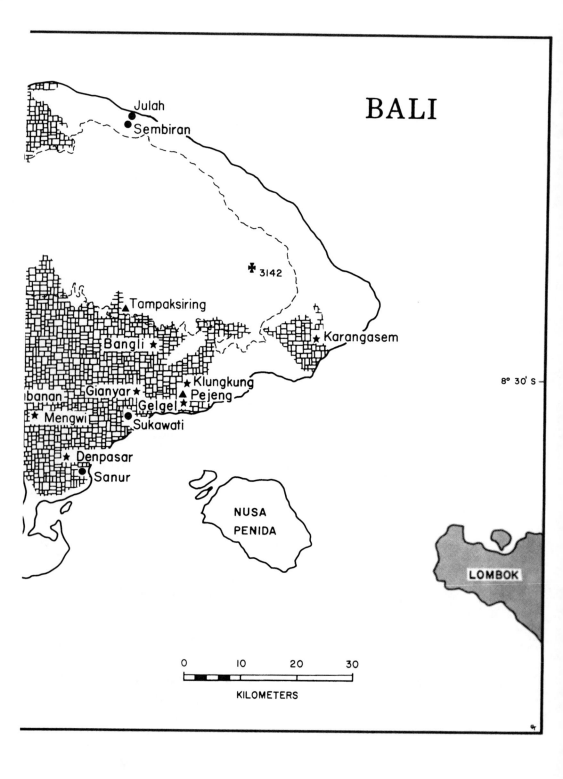

BALI

Julah
Sembiran

✠ 3142

▲ Tampaksiring

Bangli ★

★ Klungkung
Gianyar ★ ▲ Pejeng
ibanan Gelgel ★
★ Mengwi ● Sukawati

★ Denpasar
● Sanur

NUSA
PENIDA

LOMBOK

8° 30' S

0   10   20   30

KILOMETERS

CPSIA information can be obtained at www.ICGtesting.com
Printed in the USA
236077LV00005B/17/P